THE
Sacrificial Lamb

WHY GOD ALLOWED THE HOLOCAUST

Joey W. Kiser

iUniverse, Inc.
Bloomington

The Sacrificial Lamb
Why God Allowed the Holocaust

iUniverse books may be ordered through booksellers or by contacting:

iUniverse
1663 Liberty Drive
Bloomington, IN 47403
www.iuniverse.com
1-800-Authors (1-800-288-4677)

Because of the dynamic nature of the Internet, any web addresses or links contained in this book may have changed since publication and may no longer be valid. The views expressed in this work are solely those of the author and do not necessarily reflect the views of the publisher, and the publisher hereby disclaims any responsibility for them.

Any people depicted in stock imagery provided by Thinkstock are models, and such images are being used for illustrative purposes only.

Certain stock imagery © Thinkstock.

ISBN: 978-1-4759-3462-5 (sc)
ISBN: 978-1-4759-3461-8 (hc)
ISBN: 978-1-4759-3463-2 (e)

Library of Congress Control Number: 2012911316

Printed in the United States of America

iUniverse rev. date: 7/10/2012

Contents

Preface

THIS BOOK IS DEDICATED primarily to two groups of people: the Jewish people and the Muslims. Not just these two but to all who have wondered why God allowed the Holocaust to happen. This book should reveal the answers to the questions about the most horrible time mankind has ever witnessed.

Most of those Jewish people who suffered through this time are now gone, but this book should bring comfort to their descendants by explaining why the Holocaust happened. The Jewish people may now feel content as they begin to understand the reason God allowed this horrible time to happen to them.

For thousands of years the Jewish people have endured many atrocities, one after the other: torture, beatings, starvation, ridicule, mental cruelty, and murder, and a number of other overwhelming hardships. Why have the Jewish people been subjected to this treatment? Why them instead of any other race of people? Why did they have to be persecuted and falsely hated for such a long, long time?

Has God taken a special hatred toward them? Has God forgotten them? Has God turned His head away from their cries of anguish and despair? The answer to all these questions is no. God has not forsaken them. He has heard their cries and knows their pain and how they have suffered. He knows their character as a strong, humble, determined, and forgiven people. These traits are what made God decide they should be His chosen people. He chose them to bear the ultimate sacrifice so mankind would not perish from the earth. This book should explain why.

Jesus Christ was a Jewish man who chose to give his life on the cross to die for the sins of all of mankind. The Jewish people were also chosen to play a role to save mankind—not to suffer and die for the sins of mankind but to suffer and die for another reason. The purpose was so that mankind would not destroy itself in a completely different Holocaust. God chose the Jewish people, as a whole, to become the sacrificial lambs so mankind would not perish from the earth.

It is so plain to me. I just wish people could open their eyes and see what I see. But to do this one must remove all bias and prejudice from one's heart and mind. One must be honest with oneself and accept the truth openly. When will the world develop an open mind without any false thoughts to disrupt the harmony of what is real and authentic? The inability to be truthful and honest with one's own self is why there is so much sin in the world. The many problems the world faces can be resolved if only the truth is accepted.

When hate takes root in the mind, it poisons it. Then false thoughts are easily created. This can be cured only with love, flowing like the rivers and drowning out the unsound cogitations of ignorance, creating a stream of new reason and understanding that leads into the canal of intelligence. When the seeds of hate are left unchecked, they can grow to be enormous, which can barricade the intellect and turn an individual into a violent, uncaring monster. Seeing the truth is the only antidote to the soul being devoured by sin and hate.

To be honest with oneself, one must overcome the pride in one's heart. Pride is the primary element in all people that prevents the truth from being accepted. To remain right with God, people need to have control of their pride. We must know when to admit to ourselves these wrong things and then ask for forgiveness.

Most of the evil in the world is done by people who can't see the truth. They are plagued with hate, lust, prejudice, deception, power, and even religion. If mankind is ever going to find peace in this world, it must find the truth. Once truth is established in the minds of the world, the falsehoods and deceptions will wither away and die.

When prejudices are revealed, the light of veracity will shine bright, create the mirror of truth, and expose the ugliness of hate. Those who hate others need to view themselves in the mirror of truth. It is here that they can see how mean and awful they are. When people can see themselves and dislike what they see, they will begin to feel the unrest they have in their hearts about who they really are. It is here that the change comes about. The truth is simple to see, but most people who have hate imbedded in their hearts will deny the facts and lie to themselves.

When a man lies to himself and distorts the truth, he hurts only himself. When this happens, he sets himself up to destroy not just his character but also his soul and then his life.

When readers can read every word of this book while keeping an open mind, without bias, they will learn a lot about themselves and benefit greatly. They will then have the insight of seeing the real world with a better perception and with much more understanding.

People from all walks of life are searching for the truth and want to know the true meaning of life, to find God, live a happy life full of love and joy, and go to heaven when they die.

We all want the same basic things in life: a secure job and a good financial outlook for the future, and to be happy.

We all desire wealth and good health. In our minds we have a compelling passion to have what others around us have. We all want nice things and want to live a happy, healthy life, but there are many things out there in the world that prevent us from achieving those goals. The biggest one I can see is the inability to see clearly and not allow our minds to think about false things. Our minds manufacture many falsehoods, which then develop into lies and deceptions. I guess we all encounter this from time to time. I hope all those souls who read this book will open their minds and hearts and try, just try, to finish reading it before the demons of deception and duplicity enter your mind and trick you into putting it down and not finishing it.

There are many different people in the world, many religions, and many races and creeds, but we are all the same in the eyes of God.

To understand the world, one must accept that there are many different religions. The leaders of these religious groups should especially keep their minds open when they read this testament. I hope they will have an honest heart along with a patient attitude about finishing it.

Men in high places are more responsible to the flock of individuals they lead. Men in these high places will be held to a higher account for what they do. They will be rewarded by their Creator for the truth they bestow on the many who look up to them for spiritual guidance.

They also will be punished by God for their actions of anger, violence, and other negative indignations. God will not only punish them for bad actions but hold them accountable for inaction, for things that should have been done. Failure to correct a wrong is just as bad as, and in some cases worse than, performing actions of evil. The worst sin a man can commit is to look the other way when a wrong is committed and do nothing to correct it. Ignoring what God wants you to do will bring heavyheartedness to your soul. The lack of actions will not be excused when God judges us all.

Another thing: men in high places who have dedicated followers hold a greater responsibility for their well-being. These leaders should not allow personal grievances to influence their will to lead. Many men deceive themselves into acting violently, and then warp the minds of their flock because of personal things they are angry about.

I titled this book *The Sacrificial Lamb* because of what the Jewish people sacrificed in the Holocaust. They suffered from thirsty throats and hungry stomachs and all the misery one body can endure. These people were without a home to call their own, lived in a world that blamed them for everything, and a nation of people (Germans) who felt a hatred toward them like no other in the history of mankind. These poor old souls just wanted to live their lives in a normal way but were denied that right. To those Jewish people who gave their lives and suffered so horribly, and those who survived this most horrible time a better understanding that God has not forgotten you.

When the Islamic world reads this book, maybe they can begin to forget about the hate they have for the Jewish people—the hate they have had for 1,300 years now. What happened only seventy-seven years ago should erase this hate and give a new perception about the role the Jewish people played in keeping their world intact.

When Hitler formed the Nazi government in 1933, the stage was set to annihilate the Jewish race. Anyone who questioned their way of doing things or didn't go along with their doctrine of belonging to a master race was imprisoned or shot. When one group of people feels superior and that their way is the only way, evil has been established.

No group of people, no race, no religion, no tribe, and no assembly should dictate and try to force everyone to believe what they believe. To force people to think a certain way or worship God a certain way or live their lives a certain way is wrong. God is not a dictator! All people should believe what they want without being force to or forced not to. When force is put into action to overpower or take away someone's freedom, then evil has taken on its most destructive form: the idea to impose their will on others and rule.

History shows that men have tried to impose their will on their fellow man since the dawn of time. When this happens, man becomes an instrument of the Devil.

For all men to live in this world and be free has got to be God's ultimate wish for His creations. He doesn't want people to worship Him through forceful ways. He wants us to come to Him freely and without pressure.

God is not a religion. God is God. Religion is something man has created—a way to live and be associated with God. This is why people are at odds with each other: followers of every religion think theirs is the only way.

Some people belong to religious groups just so they can feel superior toward others. When people start to feel this way, God becomes distant. The religion starts to take on another role, the role of segregation. I guess that is why the world is in such turmoil. When people start to feel better or superior toward others, pride takes over the heart. When the heart is taken over by pride, any group can easily manipulate the soul. There will always be different religions in the world, but until all religions can show each other enough respect and tolerance, violence and chaos will be active.

There have always been battles going on in the conscience of mankind. Many struggles are ones humanity has been involved in since the beginning of time, such as good versus evil, freedom versus slavery, and believing in God versus the decision not to believe in God.

We all want to feel close to God. We all want to go to heaven when we die. We all want to belong in the world and be happy, but as long as people are deceived into hating others, mankind will struggle to be close to God.

When evil takes form and goes into action, some will be asked to sacrifice what they hold dear to prevent this evil from succeeding. Some will be asked to give up material things, others will be asked to give up more meaningful things. During the Holocaust a whole race of men, women, and children were chosen to give everything so the world would be saved; they were the Jewish people.

When Hitler invaded Poland in 1939, he put into action the worse institution of evil the world has ever seen. He orchestrated a regime aimed at enslaving first the people of Poland and then all the people of Europe. He would have enslaved the world if he had won the war. But he did not win the war. He did not enslave the world. His doctrine of fascism did not overpower the world because there were those who made the sacrifices needed to overcome this monstrous dictator—brave men and women who fought back and defeated the German war machine.

Making a sacrifice for others is something individuals choose to do. What happened in the Holocaust is something the Jewish people didn't choose. God made that decision. God decided to sacrifice them. God has an obligation to tell the remaining Jewish people why they had to be sacrificed. They need to be told why they had to suffer and die. This book is a testament to explain why.

This book is also to educate those who are uninstructed in God and his teachings, to reveal things that have happened that need to be known and not forgotten. I do this by explaining things easily, in a nutshell, so the reader doesn't have to read large volumes of text to learn what has happened. Telling the world in this more concise fashion will make it easier to know God and dissolve some of the hate. God is real to all people, not just the religious.

If a Muslim hates a Jewish person just because he is Jewish, then he isn't a true Muslim. If an Arab hates a Jewish person just because he is Jewish, then he doesn't know God. If any religious group hates other human beings because their beliefs are different from theirs, they aren't doing God's will. Just because someone thinks or believes differently that doesn't give them the right to hate that person. Like I said earlier, God is not a dictator and will never be. Any group of people that makes God a dictator is *not* doing His will.

Religion is only a way to believe in God; it is not meant to be used to discriminate against, or persecute, or inflict violence on others. I don't care if someone worships God through a rock. It is not my right, or anyone's right, to persecute that individual for his or her beliefs.

When people use violence toward others because their religion is different, they are only doing the Devil's work.

If there are 100 different religions in the world, the Devil would trick them all until they all would be fighting one another, for he knows the power that religion has over someone's inner strength. When the truth is shown, all true religions should understand that we all have a right to worship God in our own way, and should respect others.

We all have a right to live on this planet. We all are God's children. We all should show tolerance toward other beliefs and believe in God as individuals and not as groups. It is hate and deception that divides the people of this world, and it is religion that puts us in these groups, thus preventing us from being individuals in the eyes of God.

I hope this testament will open the eyes not just of the Jewish people but of the whole world. Let this be a time to understand—a time to open the minds and hearts of all of mankind so the truth will lead us all to a better place. Then create a new world—a world full of love and people caring for one another, a world ready to forgive and be forgiven, a world ready to see a new era of kindness, joy, and understanding.

One day all religions will adapt and begin to accept a level of tolerance long enough to embrace each other. When they develop a mutual respect for each other, the new beginning will have begun.

When the world realizes the role the Jewish people played in saving the world, the world will unite and show the Jewish people a special love. This might sound silly, but the Islamic world will usher in this new, wonderful time! I can see the Islamic world embracing the Jewish community in a most profound, majestic way. When the deceptions that have been placed on the Jewish race exposed the prejudice that feeds the hate will die off. And when the world ushers in this most wonderful time, the Islamic world will be at the very front with an expression of excitement and a profound joy in their hearts. When these things come to pass, there will be no more wars, or rumors of wars. Mankind will live in peace for a thousand years. This will happen! It is the purpose of this book.

CHAPTER 1

The History of the Jewish Race

THIS CHAPTER SHOULD TELL a little about the Jewish people. One has to ask, Why have the Jewish people been treated so horribly by the world? Their history is of a humble people, a people who have been treated viciously just because they are Jewish. This group of people has a long history of prevailing. These people who have survived many trials and tribulations have overcome the forces of evil better than any other race of people. Hate, murder, torture, hunger, thirst, and treachery—the list goes on. Also, they have become the perfect scapegoat for all of man's ills. Their pure stature and strong character and inner strength have been recorded throughout history as a struggling wonderment to survival.

When talking about the history of the Jewish people, one must start with Abraham. He is the one who started it all. I could write an entire book on Abraham and his teachings, but I shall write only about the most important things he did and a little about who he was as a man.

Around 4000 BCE Abraham was born. Nobody knows for sure the exact date, or where he was born, but scholars think it was somewhere in present-day southern Turkey or maybe Iraq. He journeyed until he came upon Canaan. This is where he dwelled for a long time. Abraham is the first man who believed that there is one God and one God only. He prayed to God every day and developed one of the most profound personal relationships with God that has ever been recorded.

Abraham was the beginning force that forged three of the most popular religions. He was the great patriarch of the Hebrew Bible. This man who gained favor from God began the Jewish race as we know it. Christians study the teachings of Abraham, who is in the Bible. It is he who brings into focus that there is one God. This spiritual element changes people's view to look away from idols and objects in the sky and develop their own personal relationship with God. Even Muslims look to Abraham as a spiritual leader and the architect of the Koran, the book they use to find their own relationship with God. There are many ways, or many religions, through which to find God, but Abraham is the one who identified God as one being.

Next are Abraham's children Ishmael and Isaac. It is these two sons that have divided the world into Jewish and Arab.

Abraham is old and still without any sons after returning from Egypt. Sarah, his wife, knows how badly her husband wants children and decides to let her maid Hagar be a surrogate mother for him. She gives her maid to Abraham, and the two engage in the act of fornication. It is not told how many times they have each other, but eventually Hagar gets pregnant and gives birth to Ishmael.

While Hagar is pregnant, Sarah grows rebellious toward her. Sarah's jealousy grows like a weed in moist soil. Every day she despises her rival and tempers fly, but she manages to put up with her.

Ishmael is born, and Abraham now has a son. The Bible says he is eighty-six years old. But dates and ages are not necessarily accurate for anyone in this time. Nobody knows exactly what a year is. But it is clear that Abraham is very old.

Thirteen years later, God orders Abraham, who is still called Abram, to circumcise himself, then Ishmael, then every other male. This act becomes the most notable feature of Abraham's life. With this, God demands that all males be circumcised no longer than eight days after birth. It is here that God changes Abram's name to Abraham, which means "father of many nations."

Many years pass after Ishmael is born when Sarah gets pregnant. The many years of jealousy and envy she has toward Hagar conjure up the spiritual juices to make her fertile. She gives birth to Abraham's second son and names him Isaac.

After Isaac is born, she totally rebels against Hagar and Ishmael. She doesn't want Ishmael to inherit what she thinks Isaac should get, so she talks Abraham into getting rid of both of them. Abraham reluctantly agrees and has Hagar and Ishmael go into exile.

It is here that the story gets interesting. The reader must understand something first: just because the Bible or any other religious text says "God said this" or "God said that," it doesn't mean God had anything to do with that verse. The scriptures are written by man, not God. So when a verse says, "This is the will of God" or "God told so and so to do this or that," it doesn't necessarily make it true. God is mentioned all throughout the Bible, but not one word is mentioned about the Devil doing this thing or that thing. Let me tell you something now: the Devil is alive and doing a lot of mischief in these hard, primitive times. I would say the Devil is more involved with the people of the Bible and all other religious texts than God is. He just isn't mentioned that much.

I say this because of what God supposedly told Abraham to do with Isaac.

God said to Abraham, "Take your favorite one, Isaac, whom you love, and go to the land of Moriah, and offer him there as a burnt offering on one of the heights which I will point out to you."

God never told Abraham this! The Devil told Abraham this! I hope I'm not offending anyone, but God would never ask this of Abraham. The Devil told Abraham this because he wanted Isaac dead. He wanted to exterminate the Jewish people even before they were established.

Something must have happened a long time ago when Lucifer was cast out of heaven by the archangel Michael. It may be Michael who had something to do with the creation of the Jewish race. I don't know. All I know is that the Devil has tried all throughout history to exterminate and completely rid the planet of the Jewish people. It is here that he begins working on his wicked ambition for the first time.

The Devil tricks Abraham into taking Isaac to a quiet, desolate place to do his dirty work. The Devil's deception works very well with religious men. That is who the Devil gets to do most of his evil deeds: men who think they are righteous and perfect. The Devil's plans are ruined when God intervenes and stops Abraham from killing his only true son conceived by God's blessing.

Let me explain. When a man marries a woman, God is present and gives his blessing. That really is the main concept of marriage: to let God be the one to join two people as one. The children who come from this union are blessed and recognized by God. Abraham was married to Sarah. Abraham was not married to Hagar. The son Sarah gives Abraham is consecrated through God. The son Hagar gives Abraham is not. Ishmael is a bastard son. This union between Abraham and Hagar is not blessed by God. It is not recognized by God and is not sanctified by God. Bastard children are children born without God's blessing. I know that might upset many who are reading this, but the truth should be recognized and told. I'm not saying bastard children shouldn't be born; all I am saying is that if a man and woman who engage in the sex act bring a child into the world and aren't married beforehand, they have created a human being without God's blessing.

My personal opinion (and since it is my book, I can write anything I want to) is that Sarah made a big mistake by allowing her maid Hagar to sleep with Abram in the first place. If you are married, neither the man nor the woman should allow anyone to come between the union God has joined and blessed.

There has been a lot of hoopla about Abraham sacrificing Isaac for God. I can't believe people can be so naïve. Think about it. Why would God want Abraham, or anyone else for that matter, to kill another human life just so He could get some joy out of it? God is not like that. God is a loving, caring spirit who wants only the best for His creations. God would never ask Abraham to kill Isaac or murder him.

This is the work of the Devil and should be addressed that way. The Devil's only power over God is deception. As long as he can deceive, he can do evil in this world. Abraham was deceived into thinking he was supposed to kill Isaac, but God intervened and stopped it. People need to use their common sense when God is involved. People should ask, "Would God really want me to kill someone just for the hell of it?" The answer is no. God is God. God would never ask anyone to do things like this. Remember, the Devil can masquerade as God and even proclaim he is God so you will do what he wants. Don't get caught up with religion so much that you lose sight of who God is and what God would want. Always be on the lookout for the Devil and his deceiving ways.

On the other hand, God may have had another plan. To get in the mind of God, one must study who God is and what He would do based on past experiences. He may have wanted to start a new righteous breed of man, a race of people conceived through His divine blessing. Now that Sarah has given Abraham a son, God may have wanted to sacrifice Ishmael instead of Isaac, since Ishmael was a bastard son and not a glorified son through the blessings of God. God may have wanted Ishmael killed so the race of Abraham would be pure and right.

At one time, maybe, God wanted Abraham to sacrifice Ishmael instead of Isaac. When He realized later that this was a mistake, He told Abraham not to do this act. I think the Devil had something to do with this scene. The Devil wanted Isaac dead, not Ishmael. Then the kin of Abraham would not live and would bring into being the race of people who will one day destroy Satan's plans to rule the world. I think the Devil manipulated what God said and deceived Abraham so that he would do the opposite.

Now getting back to Isaac. The Devil fails in his goal of killing him. Isaac goes on to procreate, ensuring the lineage of the Jewish people. With his wife, Rebekah, he has twin sons, Esau and Jacob.

Before Isaac dies, he prepares to give his blessing to his firstborn, Esau, to receive his inheritance.

Back in biblical times the firstborn sure got a lot of attention. In this case Esau and Jacob are born as twins. They both should be looked on as firstborn. They were born the same day, but since Esau came out first, he is looked at as the firstborn. This should not make any difference, but boy, does it ever.

Rebekah's favorite son is Jacob. For some reason she loves Jacob a lot more than Esau. She tricks Jacob into robbing Esau of his birthright.

The Devil once again is up to no good. He seems to have a way of warping people's thoughts and persuading them to do his mischief.

When Isaac gives his blessing to Jacob, he thinks he is giving it to Esau. Isaac is old and doesn't see very well. When the blessing is over and Esau finds out about the deception, he is mad as hell. He goes after Jacob with fire and vengeance in his eyes and murder in his heart.

Rebekah realizes she has made a terrible mistake, a mistake that might cost Jacob his life. She tells Jacob to leave town before Esau finds and kills him. So there goes his inheritance, all of it.

Jacob takes off and leaves for twenty years. While he is gone, he comes across a small tribe. There he meets a young girl, Rachel, and falls in love with her. He wants to marry her, but her father, Laban, doesn't agree to it. He has another daughter, Leah, who is older. It is customary for the older daughter to marry first. Laban likes Jacob and wants him to stay and work for him, so he devises a plan to keep him around awhile. He tells Jacob he can marry Rachel if he will work for him for seven years. Jacob must love Rachel greatly, because he agrees to this contract.

Seems like a long time to me, but when a man is young and in love, nothing will keep him from the woman he desires.

After seven years, Jacob gets to marry his longtime love—or at least he thinks he does. Laban gets Jacob drunk, and Leah, with veils over her face concealing who she really is, allows Jacob, under the cover of darkness, to engage in the sex act. When light comes and Jacob wakes up from his slumber, he looks over to the woman beside him. He realizes he has been tricked. It is Leah, not Rachel, with whom he has engaged in sex.

Mad as hell, Jacob runs straight to Laban and they have a talk. After their little talk, Laban convinces Jacob that now that he has taken away Leah's virginity, he must remain married to her. He tells Jacob that their custom is for the oldest daughter to marry first. He doesn't want to lose Jacob. Jacob has worked hard for him, and Laban doesn't want him to up and leave. He sees how angry Jacob is, so he allows him to marry Rachel. But he gets Jacob to work for him another seven years.

Most men would have just left and forgotten about the whole mess. But Jacob, still in love with Rachel, agrees to Laban's offer and works for his father-in-law for seven more years.

There is one thing I must say about Jacob: he may not be the smartest man in the world, but he sure is determined to get what he wants. To labor fourteen years just to get the woman he loves shows he is a man who possesses a strong conviction and a dedication to a profound struggle for love.

After twenty years he decides to go back and make peace with his brother, Esau. He does, and they reconcile their differences and live in peace with each other.

My summary of Jacob and Esau is this: To avoid the kind of trials and tribulations these two men encountered, you must not be greedy. Greed is one of the seven deadly sins. To want something so badly that you must lie and deceive is only going to hurt you in the long run. If Jacob had not tricked his father into giving him his brother's inheritance, he would never have had to leave his family. By doing so he got nothing. The fact that he had to toil many years to get the hand of his love was a result of the trickery of his father-in-law. Jacob in turn experienced a backlash because of his own trickery. He would have received some of Isaac's estate, but because of greed and the deceptive advice of his mother, Rebekah, he got nothing but anguish. And Rebekah, who loved Jacob so much, was left without her son. When Jacob had to leave her house, Rebekah also suffered heartbreak. The most important part of her life was taken away from her, and was taken away because of her actions and sinful ways.

A mother should love all her sons the same. Try hard not to show favorites, because when you do, you might get caught up in a web of distractions and deceit. In the long run, the one you showed more love may leave and be gone like the wind, never to return. Then you will be left alone, living with the misery of yearning for that love you once had.

Sin is a self-inflicted, shameful act that will grow to make your life miserable. God doesn't want us to sin because of what that sin might do to us in the long run. God doesn't want any of us to suffer more than we have to unless He has a reason for it. He is a God of love. He wants only the best for us. But when greed or lust or envy or pride or gluttony enters our hearts, the Devil begins to alter our thoughts to trick us into doing something that will in the long run make us miserable or destroy our lives. That is why we must admit our sins early, so we don't continue with more lies and deceit that will eventually lead to our demise.

When Jacob tricked his father, Isaac, into giving him his blessing, or inheritance, he should have asked Esau for his forgiveness and made it right with him. He would have had to put his pride on a shelf and allow for his punishment, whatever it may have been. At least he would not have had to run away from the fear of Esau killing him. If you choose to sin, make sure you are ready to ask for forgiveness. If you aren't, be ready to suffer the consequences, because there will be some.

Leah gives Jacob four sons, but Rachel gives him none. So Rachel does like Sara did for Abraham: she gives him her maid to have more children.

They did a lot of that in biblical times.

As time goes on, it is said that Jacob has two wives, Leah and Rachel, and two concubines. Jacob gets ten children from Leah and his concubines, but none from Rachel. Then finally Rachel gets pregnant and has a son. His name is Joseph.

Joseph grows up to be an outcast among his older brothers. They dislike him with a passion—I guess since he was the firstborn son of Rachel, the only woman Jacob truly loves, and because he is Jacob's favorite. Favoritism sure did cause a lot of problems back then.

Rachel later has another son. His name is Benjamin.

Jacob, now called Israel, favors Joseph more than all his other sons. He makes him a coat of many colors. He gives this to Joseph as a special token of his love. When the other brothers witness this, their jealousy grows viciously in their hearts. They talk among themselves, and the hate that was started grows and grows until it is at fever pitch. This act of love from Israel (Jacob) toward his favorite son evolves into a storm of aversion and envy from the rest of his family.

The brothers plot at first to kill Joseph, but Reuben, the oldest, will not tolerate it. He is the one who prevents the others from murdering Joseph. He still dislikes Joseph as much as the others do; he just won't tolerate any bloodshed. But Reuben has a plan just as mean.

Reuben, along with his other brothers, decides to throw Joseph into a dry well and leave him there overnight as a punishment. After they throw Joseph into the well, they sit around and joyfully listen to him scream and holler. He screams and hollers for hours and hours for someone to get him out. At first they enjoy hearing the cries of their brother, but as the hours go by, their happy state turns sour. The brothers listen to the helpless cries from Joseph until they can't stand to hear his screams anymore. They rescue him from his torturous black prison, all except Reuben.

Seeing what they have done, they know they cannot let Joseph go back and tell their father about their wicked deed. So they take him to a place where they can sell him as a slave. They sell him to the Ishmeelites for twenty pieces of silver.

When Reuben comes around the next day, he wants to know what happened to Joseph. The brothers tell him what they did. He becomes angry with them for their stupid actions. Being the oldest, he will have to tell his father about Joseph. He thinks up a lie. He and his brothers kill a goat and pour the blood on Joseph's coat. They take the coat to their father and tell him that Joseph is nowhere to be found.

Israel (Jacob) must want to die. His firstborn son from the only woman he truly loved is dead. He mourns horribly. He cries out to God, asking why his son had to die. He sobs, and goes through a very terrible time.

But Joseph isn't dead. He is sold again to another slave master in Egypt. Here Joseph gets Pharaoh's attention by interpreting his dreams.

Pharaoh tells Joseph that he is on the bank of the Nile River and sees seven fat cows. He then sees seven thin cows eat up the seven fat cows, but the thin cows stay thin. He then tells Joseph he sees seven ears of corn, large and full. Then he sees seven thin ears of corn devour the seven good ears, but they remain thin. Joseph tells Pharaoh that the two dreams are one. He says the seven fat cows are seven years of plenty and the seven thin cows are seven years of famine. He goes on to say that the seven years of famine will overtake the seven good years.

Then he tells Pharaoh to store up grain in the seven good years so there will be plenty of food to go around when the seven bad years come. Pharaoh rewards Joseph and makes him the overseer for all of Egypt.

Then when the years of famine come to pass, Egypt is rich with grain. People from all over the region come to Egypt to buy grain. Along with all the hungry people, Israel's (Jacob) sons come to Egypt to buy grain. Joseph spots them and accuses them of being spies. He first puts them in prison and then calls for them.

He is still angry with them for what they did to him. So he hatches a plan to see if they are sorry for what they did.

He holds one of them hostage until they can bring their other brother, Benjamin, to him. They go back to Canaan and tell their father what they must do. He of course strongly disagrees. He doesn't want anything to happen to Benjamin. This is the only son he had with

Rachel left. But to rescue his other son, he must let them take Benjamin back to Egypt.

When the brothers arrive in Egypt, they go to where their brother is being kept. Joseph tries to conjure up the nerve to forgive his brothers, but he can't. He must find a way to see if his brothers are worthy of forgiveness. He makes up a plan to see how much they are willing to sacrifice.

The brothers show Benjamin to Joseph to assure him that they weren't lying. Joseph gives them food and drink and listens to them talk behind the wall where he isn't seen.

When they are ready to leave, Joseph has one of his staff put a gold cup in the satchel on Benjamin's donkey. As they try to leave, the cup is shown and all the brothers are taken back to Joseph. He accuses them of stealing it and orders Benjamin to stay.

Joseph wants to know how much their brother is worth to them.

All the brothers beg and plead to Joseph not to take their brother from them. They tell him their father will surely die if they don't bring Benjamin back. They are willing to stay and be his slaves if he will let Benjamin go. Joseph is touched by their sincerity. He then pulls off his wig and tells the men that he is Joseph, their brother.

I am sure this is an emotional time for all. They hug one another, and tears flow like a river. They reconcile the past and forgive one another for all their transgressions. It must have been a very touching and moving event.

They go back to Israel (Jacob) and tell him the good news. They bring him back with his household, and they all live in Egypt happily ever after.

My summary of Joseph and his brothers is this: Joseph was hated by his brothers, and after they threw him into a dry well and then sold him to be a slave, you would think he could never forgive them. But he did. He did because he was a good man. His character was of strong merit. But he had to see first what price they would give for their younger brother. They told Joseph they would remain as his slaves just so Benjamin could go home; it was this act of love that allowed Joseph to release the hate and to forgive. Forgiveness is hard to do. One must see true repentance before the sin can be forgotten. Joseph should be revered as one of the most forgiving men, the most pure-of-heart men, in the Bible.

It is men like Joseph who give mankind a grander, more majestic, and nobler form of human being. His character is personified as a strong man of God. He represents God. He brings out God with the simple, caring love from within his heart. His soul is filled with goodness and a strong moral sense of what a righteous man should be. He is what God wants all of us to become. Joseph was a true man of God.

Joseph and his family live in Egypt, and the Hebrews grow in abundance.

Many hundreds of years go by, and many pharaohs go on to rule Egypt. A time of unjustness overtakes the land. The pharaohs put the Hebrews into slavery. Once again the Devil tricks man into enslaving the world. He does this for about 430 years. The Hebrews, or Jewish people, suffer and struggle to build Pharaoh's cities, but at a horrible price. Their blood is shed without mercy. The Devil has an upper hand in their enduring saga. The pain of the whip and the humiliation of an unjust world have the Jewish people asking God to send a deliverer, one who will rid them of the toil of deprivation and drudgery in their inequitable, unfair situation. They pray for one who will deliver them from the chains of bondage.

It is time to tell about the man who came to the aid of the Hebrew slaves: a man of God, a man who used the power of God like no other man in the Bible. He freed the Hebrews when they were slaves to Pharaoh. You cannot tell the history of the Jewish people without telling the story of Moses.

Sometime around 1400 BCE, Moses freed the Hebrews from Egypt and began the search for the promised land.

The time is not exact but is close. It is very difficult to assign an exact time to anything that is written in the Bible or other ancient religious texts, because no one knew what a year was back then, so dates and ages would not be known precisely.

He and his flock of 25,000 wandered in the desert for forty years until they found the land of Canaan. But … but was Canaan the only part of the promised land? Let's begin at the beginning, the beginning of the story of Moses and the children of Israel and their journey to find the promised land.

Before they were freed, the Hebrews were slaves. They were slaves for 430 years, forced to work for the pharaohs to make bricks to build Egypt's structures. They endured and toiled long hours, doing hard, back-breaking work at the crack of the whip. They worked long and hard with only meager amounts of food to keep them going. Unable to leave Egypt, they were destined to lead miserable lives as long as they were ruled by the Egyptians. The strong character of these poor souls was formed out of this hard labor. Their sprit was strengthened by their determination to live for a better day, a day when God would send someone to free them. Their bondage only gave them a stronger faith in God. This time when the Hebrews were in bondage was a time to build their inner strength and make them spiritually strong so they could overcome all other obstacles lying in wait for them, and there were to be many.

When Moses was born, a terrible time was brewing. Word got out that God was to send a deliverer to free the Hebrew slaves. When Pharaoh heard this, he took the threat seriously; he decreed that all firstborn male children would be killed. What kind of people would murder innocent babies because of a rumor that a deliverer was to be born? This shows how evil the pharaohs were at this time. But the evil the Devil put into the mind of Pharaoh only backfired. The one who would deliver the children of Israel from bondage was put into a basket and floated down the Nile. The basket was found by Pharaoh's daughter, who took the baby in and raised him as her own. Moses lived in Pharaoh's house and was brought up as an Egyptian; here he grew up and saw firsthand what his people were going through.

Later on when Moses got older, the truth of who he really was came out, and did so with an act of violence. Moses saw an Egyptian whipping a Hebrew slave. Moses attacked the man, and a struggle commenced. Moses fought with the man until he killed him. Some say he murdered him, but this is false. Moses killed the man to stop the beating of the slave. Once the struggle started, Moses was defending himself as much as defending the slave. Anyway, Moses justifiably killed the Egyptian and buried him in the sand. This act revealed the news to Pharaoh that Moses was born a Hebrew slave. His life changed forever. From this point on, Moses would be compelled to free the Hebrew slaves.

This act of revolt turned Pharaoh against him. Moses was then thrown out of Egypt. He wandered the desert for many years until he found a safe haven near Mount Sinai. It was here that God communicated to him through a burning bush. God guided and directed Moses to go back to Egypt and free his people, the children of Israel.

After many years in exile, Moses got back to Egypt. He was brought to Pharaoh. Moses told Rameses II (Pharaoh)to let his people go. Of course Pharaoh would not yield to his demands, so Moses told Pharaoh that God would unleash plagues on Egypt until he let his people go.

There would be ten plagues put on the people of Egypt until Pharaoh would finally give in and let the children of Israel go free.

The first plague turned the Nile River into blood. Seven days passed, and then Moses told Rameses II to let his people go. He refused. So God unleashed the other plagues. The second was frogs, the third was lice, the fourth was flies, the fifth plague killed the cattle and livestock, and the sixth was boils, or sores, that grew on the people and brought great pain and misery. The seventh plague was hail. This plague rained down on the land with a fury never before witnessed by the Egyptians, but the hail did not fall in Goshen.

Pharaoh's heart began to soften. He asked Moses to please stop the hail and said that if he did, he would allow his people to leave. So Moses raised his staff and God stopped the hail. But soon after the hail stopped, Rameses II's heart grew hard and cold, and he decided not to let the people go. Moses raised his staff and God unleashed another plague, the eighth one: locusts. The sky grew dark and black with the flying insects. Once again Rameses II told Moses that if he would stop the locusts, he would allow his people to leave. So Moses again raised his staff and God sent a strong wind to blow the swarm of locusts away and rid the land of this horrible plague. But after the locusts were gone and everything settled back to normal, Rameses II once again reneged on his promise. He told Moses he would not let his people go.

I guess Moses was getting a little bit agitated with Rameses II. He needed to bring forth something that would break Rameses II's will and persuade him not to go back on his demands. He would show God's might once again and demonstrate to him who he was up against.

Moses was only the messenger, bringing the message of what God wanted. He was His voice. It was not Moses who was bringing these plagues but God himself. He told Rameses II to do what God wanted done or more devastating plagues would come to pass.

When Rameses II told Moses he would not let his people go, he raised his staff and the light in the sky turned black. Day after day the sky was black and dark. People were getting scared and cried out to Pharaoh to let the Hebrews go. Then on the third day of darkness, Pharaoh told Moses he could take his people but that the flocks and herds must stay. Moses disagreed with Pharaoh. He wanted to leave with all the flocks and herds. So Pharaoh once again told Moses his people couldn't leave.

Pharaoh was weakening but still had a cold, hard heart. He knew he was up against a powerful force he had never encountered before. His belief that God was speaking through Moses was real. But his heart refused to give in and allow the Hebrews to leave Egypt. There would be one more plague that God would unleash that would break Pharaoh's will.

The first nine plagues didn't get Pharaoh to change his mind. It did make him realize that he was dealing with a powerful force he had never dealt with before. He was still stubborn about letting the Hebrews leave. Only when the last plague was unleashed did Pharaoh finally give in to Moses. This plague meant that the firstborn sons in Egypt would die. Pharaoh's own son would succumb to this plague. In this time of mourning, Pharaoh gave in and decided he was up against a force greater than himself.

I am sure the Devil had a fit when he saw the Hebrews fixing to leave Egypt. His plan was to enslave the world, to deceive man into enslaving his fellow man, and to bring evil to the world, causing suffering, havoc, and distress to God's children. He wasn't going to just sit by and let freedom come to the children of Israel.

The Devil uses people like the Hebrews, or any other race of people viewed as weak or vulnerable who can easily be subjected to bias and prejudice. Once this happens, groups of men feeling superior to these inferior souls can inflict their will on them. Once they control these poor souls, the real terrible evil begins. The suppressor can now feel at ease about inflicting pain and suffering on his subjects without feeling guilty. The Devil has accomplished his purpose many times. By inflicting agony on another, one willingly destroys one's soul. Inflicting more pain slowly erases what soul they have left until all is gone. The Egyptians felt superior to the Hebrews they enslaved. They controlled them for 430 years, but now the suffering the Hebrews endured will be used to build a stronger character for a new beginning.

For this new beginning has come to the children of Israel. The long, hard times they have endured as slaves is in the past. Freedom has come to God's chosen people, a humble people whom God has chosen to one day save the world. It will take many centuries for this to happen, but the character of the nation of Israel has been created. The birth of a new nation has come to pass, and this nation will one day overthrow the power of Satan and his angels. From this nation will come one who will rid this world of the evildoers. He will bring a time of peace, joy, and happiness for its inhabitants. This time will last for a thousand years. This will come to pass! But many things and many years will come and go before the Jewish people bring forth the one who will become their Messiah.

When Moses leads his flock of 25,000 out of Egypt, he is ready to lead and guide his flock to the promised land. He knows Pharaoh could change his mind, like he did the other times, so he gathers his flock and leaves Egypt with celerity and a strong determination and zeal.

After Moses and his people are gone, the Devil works on Pharaoh's heart and mind with a vengeance. Feeling broken because he has lost his slaves, and still mourning the loss of his son, evil thoughts flood Pharaoh's mind. He wants revenge now! He wants to inflict pain and suffering and death. He wants to destroy the thing that has demeaned and humiliated him. He wants to kill Moses with a passion.

The Devil poisons Pharaoh's mind with hate. He uses the one element in a man's being that easily leads to his destruction; this element is pride. The wounded pride of losing his workers sets into Pharaoh's heart like a burning forest. His flaming desire to get back what was his takes over his mind and consumes his soul. The reality of losing anything doesn't agree with a great and powerful Pharaoh.

He makes ready to go after Moses and bring back his slaves. The Devil is in his heart, and wickedness engulfs his spirit. He sets out with a vengeance.

When Moses sees Pharaoh coming after him, he leads his people south. It is here that Moses parts the Red Sea. Some say he did it, others say he crossed the Sea of Reeds at low tide and escaped Pharaoh's army. It really doesn't matter who is right. Moses did escape Pharaoh and continued to lead the children of Israel to the promised land. I will let readers believe what is in their own mind and heart.

It is this part where the true history of the Israelites is told. I have told the story of Moses to get to this part. This is the part where God gives the Jewish people their homeland—theirs and no one else's. It is a place the Jewish people can always call home, a place where they can always go if the world turns against them, a sanctuary where they can be safe so when the evil forces of the world begin to persecute and kill them, they will have a place to go. A home so no evil could get to them. A land, a country, a holy site they could always call their own. This territory is called Israel.

About three months after Moses escapes Pharaoh's army, they are attacked by the Almalicites. The Israelites are assaulted from behind, and many are killed. The blood of the new nation has been shed, and the soil is stained with their blood. It is here where Israel forms a nation. Where a people sacrifice their lives is where their homeland is created. God gives the Israelites their country. They have fought and died on this land, so it is important to note that this is consecrated land now.

Many scholars have questioned why Moses wandered in the desert for forty years. Many an Israelite was born and died on this ground. It is easy to understand that all the land on which the Israelites were born, walked, fought, and died becomes part of their nation. When a people bury their dead on a land, and when a people bring new life on this land, and when a people fight for and die for it, that land should become theirs. By wandering around for forty years, the Israelites earned the right to claim this land as theirs. Their blood, which consecrates the ground of this territory, gives them the right to proclaim this land as part of Israel.

It is so obvious! It is so plain to see that God has given this group of people this land. They have earned it by the sacrifices they have made. The people who left Egypt are not the same anymore. They now have their own territory. They now have their own country. Not only is the land of Canaan the promised land for the Israelites but so is all the land consecrated by them. As long as babies are born, and as long as the blood of these humble people stains the ground, this land is theirs. This is the only reason I can see that God wanted Moses to take forty years before settling in Canaan.

After the Almalicites attack Moses and his new nation of followers, he knows he needs to build an army. He knows that if he is to survive, he must be ready to fight off any hostile tribes. So he begins to train an army.

His spies tell him that Canaan is well protected and he will need a large army to take it. He will need swords and other weapons to ready his army, and time to train the soldiers. He realizes that it is not time to enter Canaan. He is compelled to lead his people south. He takes them to Mount Sinai. It is here that God speaks to him again through the burning bush. Maybe he needs another talk with God about what to do next. Anyway, Moses leads his flock to the southern part of this territory at Mount Sinai.

I believe God wants to test the children of Israel to see what kind of people they really are. I believe God tests all men in His own unique way to understand them better, and to make sure they can handle other hardships that may lie ahead for them.

The hunger and thirst these people endured must have been horrible. Walking long miles of desert day in and day out had to be grueling. I am sure the complaints Moses heard on a day-to-day basis were more than he could handle. But discipline would be very important if the Israelites were to survive and grow to be a great nation.

By the time the Israelites get to Mount Sinai, resentment has reached a climatic high. The people are hungry and thirsty and tired of walking this long, dusty journey. Many want to go back to Egypt, where they had fish and fruit and meat. The promise of having milk and honey only makes the people more upset about the situation they are in. Moses knows he has to do something to make the situation better for his people, so he goes up Mount Sinai to converse with God. He is gone forty days, and when he comes down, he has with him two tablets cut out of stone. He has with him the most important set of laws ever created: the Ten Commandments.

When people are led by someone, they are more inclined to stay in line and live right. But when that leader leaves and the people have to live without being told what they should do, it is easy for them to go astray and take up bad practices. When Moses comes back, he is indignant about what he sees. The people he led out of Egypt from bondage from Pharaoh—God's chosen people, the people whom he was to make a great nation—are now worshipping a golden calf.

When he sees this, he takes the two tablets and throws them down and destroys them. He is outraged. His hate for seeing this act changes Moses forever. His fury must infuriate God. When Moses breaks the tablets containing the Ten Commandments in his hysterical rage, God becomes equally angry at Moses.

The Devil doesn't want God's testament to be shown to the world, so he plots and schemes to find a way to get the only one who could destroy the word of God: Moses. He bamboozles the Israelites into doing the one thing Moses can't stand: the worshipping of an idol. The Devil deceives the Israelites into making this golden calf just to get Moses to go into an angry fit and then destroy God's holy word.

You have to give the Devil credit on this one. He knows he has to come up with an idea to trick the Israelites to do something that will infuriate Moses to the point of destroying God's own testament. The only way these tablets will be destroyed is if Moses himself does it. The Devil is cunning and very clever about how to trick people, all people. His mastery of deception, this time, will hamper the future of the people of Israel.

It is not just throwing the tablets down and breaking the Ten Commandments that is so horrible; it is what Moses does afterward while he is still in this hateful fit.

But before I tell the reader what Moses does, it is a good time to converse about why I am writing about this time, and the reasons behind it. First, this part of the book is a place to understand who Moses and the children of Israel were. Knowing the obstacles they faced and the hardships they went through helps us better comprehend who they were. Understanding and clarifying what really happened back then is very important if one wants to learn the truth. This text isn't just to tell the story of Moses and the Israelites. It is to explain in a more realistic fashion that the real God is more loving and caring than what is portrayed in the scriptures. God is not always what some men in the Bible have written about.

Second, God is more mature and genuine than most people give Him credit for. God is a loving God. He wants only the best for His children. He isn't a man who sometimes can't control his anger and does things badly. God is in complete control all the time; it is man that isn't. God is perfect in every sense of the word.

When the Israelites were worshipping the golden calf they made, God wasn't deliriously furious at them for this ignorant act. He wasn't ready to cast them into a lake of fire or hell for this act. It is silly to think God is so weak or threatened that He would harm His children because He doesn't get worshipped. Somewhere in the scriptures someone wrote that God is a jealous God. This is a completely false misrepresentation, an attempt to degrade God somewhat. Worshipping idols or other material things hurts only the individual who is doing this silly act. Putting your faith in a physical object only warps your spirit and divides you from God. Then when you are divided from God, you can easily be led astray and be deceived by the Devil. So you only hurt yourself when you worship idols.

Back to Moses. When he talked with God and heard His voice, it did something to Moses' spirit. In his own mind he now feels better and greater than everyone else. The moralistic acts he did for God have given him the ego of a mighty, righteous man. I mean he has spoken to God with the understanding of what God wants done. This would make any man feel impregnable. He feels superior now before his enormous flock of followers. Anything he says will be done. Anything he says will be looked on as the word of God. He now can play the role of God if he wishes. Nothing Moses can do now will be looked upon as something wrong. His pride is so large, he would never admit doing anything wrong. He is right in all things now, at least in his mind. There is no force on earth that will make him admit to an error. Anything he says or does will be looked on as okay. This invincible sensation growing in his heart is now unleashed before the children of Israel. He is now the perfect individual to do the Devil's work.

This may be hard to accept, but it must be told. Moses orders the Levites to massacre more than 3,000 people as punishment for the act of idol worship of the golden calf. Moses begins to inflict harsh and cruel punishments for any infraction of the law.

The Levite tribe is Moses' personal guard. This tribe is like a secret-police force that will do things Moses asks without question—a group of people who will carry out anything, and I mean anything, that Moses wants done. He orders this group to kill without mercy the ones he thinks are responsible for any sacrilege. More than 3,000 die from this decree. Moses has become so righteous, he can do things above the law and no one will question his word.

I think this act is why God doesn't let Moses enter the promised land. It makes sense to me. Why should Moses get to see the promised land when in fact he violated one of the Ten Commandments in a most horrid manner? "Thou shalt not kill." God must have felt terrible putting Moses in charge of the Ten Commandments at this time. How could the children of Israel accept this as law when even Moses couldn't keep it? How hypocritical is this? This also may be the reason Moses wandered in the desert for forty years. He may have lost his direction with his conscience burning his soul for inflicting his vicious decrees and for intolerable impatience toward his people. Who knows? Maybe this was Moses' punishment from God for acting so self-righteous or ethically perfect. Ever since God spoke to Moses, he has felt impregnable to all others. He has become self-righteous and cruel to his people. Let's hope God doesn't speak to any other man. We don't need anyone else walking around with this profoundly superior attitude.

There is a part in the Bible where Moses strikes a rock of a mountain and water flows out. Moses takes credit for it bringing forth water. God gets mad at him for taking credit for bringing the water up. For this reason, it is said, God punishes Moses by denying him entrance to the promised land for this terrible sin. I just don't buy this silly reason. God isn't so immature that He would punish someone because He didn't get the proper recognition. This is so silly. People need to understand something: just because something is written in the Bible or any other religious text, that doesn't necessarily make it true. Man wrote these things, not God. Man is fallible, God isn't. Nobody should blindly accept everything that is written in any text in the name of God. People should let their hearts decipher what is real or not real, what is right and not right, and what could lead you to do something wrong or against what God truly wants you to do.

There is not one religious leader in the world whom the Devil can't deceive. The more religious a person is, the easier it is to trick him into using God as his instrument of evil. The more followers this person has, the stronger the pride of life will be present in his heart. Many have been led to kill, torture, and inflict evil on their fellow man because of zealous religious leaders who have been deceived or had their feelings hurt.

I hope the readers of this text will keep their hearts and minds open when they are confronted with having to do something that inflicts harm on someone in the name of God. We all will have to account for our actions in this world. No religion, no group of religious leaders, no good intentions, no amount of praying will remove you from answering to God after you die. There will be a day when you must account to God for your actions, and no man is immune to this time. Those clergy who have control over many people will be held even more accountable if they use God or God-like control to do evil and inflict violence on the world. Those who use God to trick or deceive man into doing evil will feel the full force of God's wrath for eternity.

Getting back to Moses: he finally gets his army ready and decides to fight his way to the land of Canaan. It has now been nearly forty years since the Exodus. Many tribes have fought the Israelites over the years in an effort to exterminate them, but all have failed. The children of Israel have become hardened and possess a strong army now. Now it is their time to take the land of Canaan and make it their new homeland. All they need to do is defeat the Canaanites.

Moses has died, and Joshua will now lead the Israelites. His fierce determination is needed to overcome the Canaanites. Joshua is just the right man to accomplish this endeavor.

It is somewhere around 1230 BC. Joshua fights and defeats the Ammonites, and then goes on to fight the battle of Jericho. This battle is probably the most famous of all battles in the Bible. It isn't just a battle to conquer but is one of extermination.

Joshua marches his towering army around the city of Jericho. His army numbers around 8,000–9,000 soldiers. The population of Jericho is around 2,500 to 3,000 inhabitants, and most of them are innocent civilians. Jericho is a small city.

The Bible tells us that for six days in a row, with seven priests carrying seven rams' horns proceeding with the Ark of the Covenant, Joshua's army marches around Jericho. Then on the seventh day a long blast is sounded on the horns. The army gives a mighty shout, and the walls come tumbling down. All the men advance straight ahead and take the city.

This text makes God the killer of the people of Jericho. Like magic, stone walls just fall down and kill the people. Once again the writer of this text is making God out to have magical powers to do evil. I don't buy it, and readers of this text shouldn't either. God doesn't murder people with acts of magic. This text only makes it easier to put the blame on God and not Joshua when he slaughters all the people, and he does. Joshua puts all to the sword—men, women, and children. This vicious act of savagery and brutality should not fall on God's hands, but on Joshua's and his soldiers'.

I do believe the walls came down, but only after Joshua laid siege to the city. I believe the encircling of the city for six days was a type of psychological warfare or maybe a diversion to give Joshua time to bring specially trained commandos into the city.

While Joshua was parading his army around the city, it would have been easy to lift up special forces and hide them with the help of the prostitute Rahab. It was she who helped the Israelites get troops inside the walls. She placed a red rope outside her dwelling so men could climb up. After six days of parading around the city this should have given Joshua time to place forty or so of these special forces inside the city.

On the seventh day Joshua gave the order to sound the ram horns and give the loud shout.

This could have been the signal for the special forces inside to attack and overwhelm the guards and open the gates. This small force would have given Joshua all he needed to enter and destroy Jericho.

Like I said earlier, he spares no one. All the men, women, and children are put to the sword. Then they burn Jericho to the ground. Joshua would have his victory. His first is in Canaan, but it must be made clear that God didn't murder these people and destroy their city. God must have wept to see the carnage and the blood that was shed. One wonders who was in charge of the Israelites, God or Joshua. God would never have done this to the people of Jericho. War brings out the worst in man. In this case the Israelite army has done its worst.

The next engagement in front of Joshua is the battle of Ai.

Joshua sends a reconnaissance group to gather information in the city of Bethel. Bethel was a named after the Canaanite tribe the Bethelites. This city is a strategic importance to conquering Canaan.

As the group of 600 or so troops paces the territory, they come to the ruined city of Ai. A thousand years earlier Ai was a very big and populated city, but now it is a city of broken walls and caved-in buildings. As the men enter the ruined city of about fourteen acres, the Bethelites come out from their hiding places and attack the Israelites. A fierce battle takes place! It is here that the Bethelites get their revenge for what the Israelites did to Jericho. Most are killed, but a few manage to fall back and then get back to Joshua. When they tell Joshua of this defeat, he makes ready for his army to go back to Ai. With revenge in his heart and murder in his eye, he is determined to destroy the Bethelites and leave them crushed. This is Joshua's first defeat in Canaan.

His spies tell Joshua the Bethelites have an army of around 2,500 men, so he makes plans to use his 8,000-man army to destroy them. He does this with cunning cogitation. He doesn't want to show the Bethelites his entire army. He doesn't want to scare them off and have to fight them in a long, drawn-out, one-on-one campaign. He wants to draw them out into the open so he can destroy them.

When Joshua gets to Ai, he places only 1,000 men on the front of the Bethelites' army. They think this is the entire Israelite army and attack. The Bethelites inflict great casualties among the Israelites. The Israelites run away in hopes that the Bethelites will pursue them, and they do. They even send their reinforcements to rally and destroy the fleeing army. When they do, Joshua signals his army to attack from the rear and the front. The Bethelites are caught in the middle. They are decimated! They are all put to the sword and killed, except the king of Bethel. He is hanged in a tree right in front of the city. The city soon surrenders without any more bloodshed.

The innocent blood that must be shed in war is common in this time. There are no prisons to put any prisoners in. There is no food to feed them. There is no one to look after them. The thought of children growing up with revenge in their hearts is something that cannot be tolerated. War is brutal and cruel. But to have victory one must do things that are harsh and sometimes cruel.

Joshua is getting stronger and bolder with victory after victory. His eye now is on Gibeon. He defeats five Canaanite tribes at one of the famous battles of the Bible: the battle of the Eglon Valley. He drives his army thirty miles in two days to get to the right point for the battle to take place. Here at Gibeon he charges his army down the hill with the sun on their backs, blinding the Canaanites and soundly defeating them.

Joshua goes on and defeats thirty-one tribes of the Canaanites. But he like Moses will die before he can enter the promised land.

But soon the children of Israel will have their new homeland. The land of milk and honey will be theirs. This large magnitude of people will break up and form twelve tribes. These are their names:

Gad, Manasseh, Issachar, Asher, Maphtah, Dan, Ephraim, Benjamin, Judah, Reuben, Simeon, Zebulun.

Many men and women are of significant historical value to the Jewish race; they fought hard and preserved Israel so it could become a great nation. Here are a few of them.

In the Bible at the time of the Judges there was one man who proved to be a strong, courageous warrior and leader. His name was Gideon. He was born in the Manasseh tribe around 1100 BC.

This is a lawless time for the Israelites. The tribes have become distant from the others. There is nothing to unite them as one people. Like the Old West, justice is handled out hastily and many times without fairness. The one who uses his sword quickly is the one who usually prevails.

For seven years a violent tribe wreaks havoc on the Israelites. They come out of the Arab desert and are called the Midianites. It is here that Gideon shows his true colors and devises a way to defeat this menace to his people.

He fights his enemy in small groups of fighters. He trains and commands 300–600 special team forces to sneak in and attack his enemies quickly.

In one battle involving the Midianites, he gives them the impression of a large force attacking by encircling them and showing torches under the cover of darkness. He leaves one area open so the forces he is fighting will have this one way to escape. Then as the frightened forces flee the battle area, the main body of the Israelite army will be waiting for them. In other words, he gives the impression that the main force is attacking, and then chases them to an area where they think they can escape. Here the main army will be waiting in the dark for them. Here the enemy will run into a wall of destruction. Gideon's plan defeats the Midianites.

After the battle, Gideon isn't satisfied. The king of the Midianites has escaped the battle. Gideon knows the Midianite forces will grow back if the king is still alive, so he passionately chases after him. When he catches up with him, he wants to humiliate him by having his son kill him. He gives the sickle-shape sword to his son and tells him to behead the king. His son walks up to the king but can't seem to gather the courage to kill the man. So Gideon takes a sword from one of his men and beheads the king with a mighty blow.

After all the Midianites are killed and no longer pose a threat, Gideon quietly disappears from the stage of violent confrontation and lives a long, peaceful life.

Not only were Jewish men important military commanders in the creation of Israel, but women too played an important role in this endeavor. One of those women was named Deborah.

It is around 1100 BC, and Deborah is like the Joan of Arc of her day. She plans and studies ways to destroy enemies of the Israelites.

At this time there is a threatening tribe called the Philistines. They are a sea people who swept down the Mediterranean Sea and settled at the southern part of Canaan. It is not known how long these people have been here, but it is long enough to pose a threat to the Israelites. The Philistines have chariots, so it is believed that they have been in this area quite a long time; to build chariots takes time and a lot of copper and tin. And they have hundreds of chariots with which to wreak havoc on the Israelites.

There is a man named Sisera who many think is a Philistine who commands an army that the Israelites feel threatened by. Deborah doesn't want him to join forces with the Canaanites, so she devises a plan to kill him and his army. She tricks Sisera into moving his army to Mount Tabor. With his chariots roaring to the battle, Deborah orders a general named Barak to flood the area through the drainage ditches so that when Sisera gets there, his chariots will get stuck in the mud. Barak will do battle there and destroy this army.

The battle goes well for Deborah, but the Philistines still pose a great threat to the Israelites. Their numbers are many, and the revenge that is growing in their hearts is real. The Philistines will again have their day against the children of God.

Like a virus to the body, many tribes will rise up and fight the Israelites. But their stubborn nature will overtake all their enemies like a strong antibiotic drug that kills the infection of any and all invading armies. They are a force with determination and the resolve to defeat any and all forces. This inner strength is imbedded into the soul of the people who form this great army.

The Israelites will use nature to help them defeat their enemies. They have the intelligence to use the sun and the water as their allies in battle.

The force of God is with them, but the twelve tribes of Israel still are not united. There is nothing to unite them. What they need is one man to unite them, one man to bring about one powerful country, one man to conjugate the people as one people, one man to forge the twelve tribes into one nation. What they need is a king.

Around 1020 BC the time has come for Israel to bring about a king. They choose one of the greatest military leaders of the Bible. He is a fierce warrior and a brilliant tactician. His name is Saul.

His best trait as a leader is his supreme ability to bring together the Israelites to fight their enemies. Without someone to unite the people as one strong fighting force, the Israelites would slowly be defeated. Saul proves to be a true battle-hardened captain who will show the world that he and his army will take on any force wanting to overpower them.

Saul will have an army of 12,000–14,000 regular troops along with 3,000 or so special forces. His training and supervision and discipline make this army superior for the time.

But as time goes on, Saul loses his direction with God. Saul distances himself from God and chooses a path that is not what God wants. He becomes an evil king.

All the fighting Saul has to do—and there is a lot of bloodshed done—results in his spirit being affected by all the killing. Many thousands of men are butchered and slaughtered on the battlefields. The carnage is incomprehensible. The gore and blood from thousands of people takes its toll on his mind and the heart. Saul's soul becomes stained with the blood of thousands. The meaning of life and death becomes nothing to Saul. His heart becomes evil, and he loses God's graces.

God rejects Saul as king and thinks it is time to choose someone else, to find someone after God's own heart. God tells the prophet Samuel to go out and find one who is worthy to be the king of Israel. Samuel is directed to find the man named Jesse and choose one of his sons. It is here that Samuel finds David and anoints him king.

At first Saul loves David, but soon his love turns to hate. His envy grows like a wildfire. He is jealous of David for winning over the affections of the people by killing Goliath. This jealousy will haunt Saul's mind and burn his soul.

One day Saul throws a spear at David, narrowly missing him. David leaves the city to save his life. Saul's obsession with killing David overwhelms his being. Saul, along with 3,000 men, chases after and traps David at a place called Engedi.

In a cave where Saul sleeps, David cuts off a piece of his skirt. The next day David yells down to Saul and confronts him. "Look here, Saul; I have cut this piece off your skirt while you slept. I could have well killed you." Saul looks at his skirt and sees where part of the garment is missing. He realizes David could have killed him but didn't. His heart warms up. He lifts up his voice and weeps. He tells David he is a much more righteous man than he is. The evil he felt about David is gone. Saul leads his men back home and leaves David in peace for all time.

While Saul is king, his son Jonathan kills a Philistine and starts a four-year bloody conflict. Saul, Jonathan, and his army meet their end at Mount Gilboa at the sword of the Philistines.

After 500 years of blood and violence, Israel is about to become an empire. It is now around 1000 BC, and the children of Israel will have a piece of the world they can call their own.

Soon after Saul dies at Mount Gilboa, David becomes king of Israel. He will be the light of his people like the sun is to the world. David will be like no other leader for the people of Israel. He is a man after God's own heart. He reigns as king for forty years and is loved like no other leader before or since.

I have chosen David to be my last Jewish individual to write about. He is probably the most famous Jewish man in the Bible next to Jesus. There are many others to write about, but the history of the Jewish people was established with David, so I shall end with him. To tell his story would just be redundant, because it has been told many times. I choose not to tell his story but only the philosophy surrounding him. Who was he? Why did God choose him to be king of Israel? I also address the scandals and tribulation he faced.

I shall start with the prophet Samuel, the man who anointed David as king. God leads Samuel to the house of Jesse. Jesse is a good, honest man but mainly a man with good judgment. It is important to note that God tells Samuel who to go to. The real prophets of God are led by God and not by any other means. Samuel looks over all of Jesse's sons and chooses David. His humble personality and pure heart are easy to see. Samuel anoints him king with oil and blesses David.

David then knows in his heart he has a mission to do for God. God begins at that moment to work with David through his heart and mind to make him the man He wants him to become. Because David is only a boy at this time, God is ready to start his transformation to become king of Israel.

Later on at the Eglon Valley the Philistines are conjuring up trouble. They want a fight, but the Israelites are reluctant to give them one. To provoke a fight, they send one mighty soldier to kill one of the Israelites. This soldier's name is Goliath.

I believe the Philistines do this to conjure up hate in the hearts of the Israelites. For the Israelites, seeing one of their own dead lying on the ground will bring a burning hate to their hearts, and the Philistines hope they will attack them in retaliation. If they do, the Philistines will destroy them. But things don't work out the way they planned.

David knows he will be tested. God has been working with him in His own profound and unique way, preparing him for his test. So when the Philistines challenge the Israelites, David takes up the challenge.

David, showing no fear, stands alone on the hot, dusty field of battle. Goliath, standing like a tower, grins at David as the two walk toward each other.

The audience with great anticipation gathers around to view the confrontation that is about to take place. Laughter is heard from the Philistines' side as their nine-foot giant walks slowly toward David.

As he walks, he looks at David with evil in his eye and a delighted smirk on his face. He is like a monster ready to devour his prey. Wearing his armor and carrying his shield and sword, Goliath bellows out his words to David. He tells the meek shepherd boy he will feed his flesh to the birds. After hearing the loud, deep threat, David takes his sling and casts his first stones at Goliath. They bounce off Goliath's shield as laughter erupts from the Philistines. David once again slowly casts a stone at Goliath. Not slinging the stones hard, David continues to entice Goliath but keeps his distance. David continues to give his opponent the impression that he is weak and frail. Goliath absorbs the deception and throws down his shield. He then rushes David! David, seeing the giant coming toward him, stands steady and begins to swing his sling fast and faster until Goliath is only a few yards away. Then he unleashes his projectile with a fury. The smooth stone strikes Goliath in the head. This only knocks down the giant but doesn't kill him. As Goliath rolls around on the ground, David quickly grabs Goliath's sword and hurriedly cuts his head off.

The loud, rambunctious laughter from the Philistines' side becomes very quiet as the Israelites jump up and down and begin to chase the Philistines away. The people are joyous and happy. David has killed Goliath!

When David kills Goliath, he restores the Israelites' faith. He fortifies their inner strength with a more powerful determination. He shows them that no matter how small one is, one can defeat the enemy if only one has the courage to meet the challenge.

This young shepherd boy destroys the mighty giant with only a sling and five smooth stones. This strong trait of courage is embedded in the hearts and minds of the men of Israel. David has shown his courage; now he must show his ability to lead. And to do this, he must win over the hearts and minds of an entire nation.

It is important to note that David kills Goliath; he doesn't murder him. When someone is trying to kill you, you have the right to defend yourself and, if necessary, kill the perpetrator. There is a difference between killing someone and murdering someone.

When word gets out that David has killed Goliath, he becomes a hero. Everyone loves David, everyone except Saul. Saul becomes very jealous of David and eventually tries to kill him. It really is funny how jealousy can consume a man's heart and literally destroy his soul. This is the case with Saul.

Saul and his son Jonathan meet their end at Mount Gilboa, and David is made king by the elders in Judah. But the violence does not end here.

Saul has another son. His name is Ishbosheth. For two years civil war rages between David and Ishbosheth.

This time is a time of murder and blood. To unite the nation as one, Ishbosheth has to be defeated. David invites Abner, Ishbosheth's main general, to come and talk about a peace treaty. He comes and talks with David about reaching a peaceful solution, but Johab, David's main general, murders Abner. It is not known if David ordered this act, but I am sure he knew about it beforehand.

Now that Ishbosheth's main general is dead, he is without strength to fight David's armies, but not long after, Ishbosheth is murdered in his sleep. Again David may not have ordered the assassination, but it is clear he profited from Ishbosheth's death.

With all the obstacles out of the way, David is proclaimed king. At this time not all the people favor David as king. It is still an uncertain time for the Israelites. The people are still not united as one nation. Communication problems along with domestic squabbles still divide the people. In this time before telephones, televisions, and computers, uniting the nation is a slow process. It takes a long time to win over the will of the people—a very long time. But slowly the people come together.

In the forty years David reigns as king, he goes through many trials and tribulations. He goes through sex scandals and is even guilty of murder. His son Absalom rebels against him and dies in a violent revolt.

I chose not to write about these things because it was not David's weaknesses, or his poor judgment at times, or the webs of distractions in which he entangled himself, but the man who brought the people together and formed a great nation, a nation born of the harsh, cruel institution of slavery and many years of bloodshed.

He never had the complete devotion of the total population or did everything right, but he was a man whom God loved. He was imperfect and did things that were wrong because he was human. He lived 3,000 years ago without the uses of modern devices and still managed to keep the tribes of Israel somewhat united, and for that he is looked on as one of the greatest heroes of the Bible and of the Jewish community.

David was like the carbon atom to conjoin the people and transform twelve tribes into one molecule. This one molecule metamorphosed into a new element to form the foundation of a land that all Jewish people could call home. This new element would turn dirt into a great land and turn regular people into a magnificent society. This society will one day create one that will overthrow the Devil and his angels. This small territory will be a community that one day will strengthen the spirit of every nation on the planet and form a union to bring peace for a thousand years. This all will happen one day. This molecule, this element, this driving force, this territory, this spirit, this community of the Jewish race: this nation called Israel.

CHAPTER 2

Why the World Has Hated the Jewish People So Much

IF THE DEVIL IS to win the souls of men, he must devise a plan to make the hearts of men evil. To do this, he will use hate to possess and control the mind and heart. Hate is the element that is essential to devour the soul. The deception to make one hate is the primary staple to induce the appetite to win over souls. It is hate that has tricked mankind into looking for a scapegoat for all the problems of the world.

The Devil has devised a plan to kill all the Jewish people because of his hate for this race of people. He has wanted them dead ever since Abraham was walking the planet. Satan has forged the world carefully so that when his son the Antichrist comes into the world, his plan will be most effective.

The Jewish people will be the Devil's primary element to turn men against one another. It is hate that turns men into monsters. If Satan is to win the souls of men, he must make mankind hate. It is hate that burns a man's soul to ashes. It is the Devil's main tool to enslave man and then destroy him. The Jewish people will be used to conjure up as much hate as possible so the Devil can win over the souls of mankind.

Since the beginning of time, evil forces have tried to enslave the world and hate has been used to accomplish this endeavor. And the Jewish people are the race upon which so much hate has been focused.

Why has there been so much hate imposed on this race of people? It is like the whole world has a reason to hate these humble people. The Jewish people have fought long and hard just to survive in the world. Why is there so much hatred for these people?

This chapter is dedicated primarily to showing the world some of the persecution the Jewish people have faced since the time of Jesus. They have been treated badly, but no matter what hardships are put on them, they never rebel against God as a whole. There is something in their nature that keeps them in tune with God. They never blame God for their hardships. They continue to keep the faith and persevere.

If given a choice to be a slave or die, the Jewish people would choose to die. They know in a way unique to themselves that if they were put in slavery, they would eventually rebel against God, blaming Him for their hardships. The Devil would then have an upper hand in trying to control the outcome of the world. If he can turn the Jewish people against God, he will have all the power he needs to fulfill his agenda. The Jewish people with their strong faith, will and love for God will be needed to keep the world intact. Their sacrifice will be called on from God. It is God who chose these people to bear the most hardships one can imagine so that mankind will not perish.

The Devil is afraid of the Jewish people. He knows if the Jewish people are alive they will one day bring into being one who will overcome the Devil and his evil ways. This is the main reason the Devil hates the Jewish people so much. He wants to destroy them so they will not usher in the one who will save the world.

The Devil also uses the Jewish people to win over the souls of man, to inflict evil and in turn surrender their souls to him. One of the primary ways the Devil wins over souls is by imposing iniquity on a race of people. Then he lets the harshness and suffering they inflict reduce their souls to black ashes. He does this by deceiving their minds with prejudice and hate. He knows these evil, violent, torturous actions they perform will in turn make others follow their lead and do the same. Many more horrible and agonizing acts will be inflicted, and more souls will be consumed.

Ever since man has walked the planet, the Devil has had a plan for us, to turn man against man, brother against brother, race against race, and religion against religion, hoping he could kill us off and enslave the rest. He wants to rule the world by empowering his dictators to do his bidding, to control all that is good and make this world a slave world. He wants to make all of mankind miserable so God will have to destroy it. Then he will take the next step and rule heaven and make God a slave. But first he must rule the world. The Jewish people will be one of his instruments in turning the world against itself.

Abraham had two sons. One son was Isaac. The other son was Ishmael. They were born not just as two sons, but evolved into two races of people. Isaac became the Jewish race. Ishmael became the Arab race. These two sons of Abraham would revolutionize the world like no other for four thousand years. How can so many people in the world become so divided by the bitterness of these two individuals? The answer is simple: deception.

When Abraham separated Isaac and Ishmael, he did so to prevent a war. It is good that Abraham had the wisdom to divide them and their tribes. He saw the conflicts the two brothers had and realized that the only way to keep the peace was to separate them. If Abraham hadn't done this, bloodshed would have followed. This is what the Devil wanted: to turn Isaac and Ishmael against each other so they would fight and kill each other. The Devil's plans were ruined for the time being.

When the Egyptians enslaved the Hebrews for 430 years, this was a time the Devil could divide and enslave some of mankind, robbing man of everything and in turn making them curse God for their misery. But it didn't work. This time of slavery only strengthened the faith of the Jewish people. The hardships and suffering just made their character strong and resilient. It gave them a stronger relationship with God, a reason to want God more, to rescue them and free them from bondage. God did this by sending Moses to their rescue, and we all know the rest. The Jewish people ended up having their homeland, Israel, and ever since then, the Devil has used this land to bring havoc to the people of this world.

One of the reasons the world hates the Jewish people is that they want their country. The evil forces of the world all want Israel, not just Jerusalem like many think, but Israel and all of it, just so the Jewish people will not be united. If the Devil can divide Israel, he can divide the Jewish people. If he can divide the Jewish people, he can continue to do his evil in the world. But when the Jewish people become united with the Arab people, Israel will be the land that will forge a new union of peace throughout the world. And the Devil will have no domain in the world. He will be defeated by his own doing. His power to deceive will no longer take hold, and the biased feelings with which he has poisoned the world will no longer work. The world will see the Jewish people with a different attitude. The world will come to love the Jewish people when they realize what they have done to preserve the world. But until they do, the Devil will continue to use the Jewish people as his instrument to bring hate into the world.

The Romans came and conquered Israel with a brute force and a collective energy that overwhelmed what the Jewish community could stand. They were now under the rule of a foreign power. The Romans ruled not just by force but with treachery and deceit. They turned the Jewish people against themselves. The Devil enjoyed this time, a time of misery and treachery for the Jewish people.

Why is there so much suffering in the world? Surely God didn't mean for so many people to have so many hardships in life. The Jewish people have surely had their share of hardships. Why is there so much hunger in the world? Why are there so many thirsty people struggling to taste clean water? Viruses creating diseases in the bodies of so many poor men, women, and children without hope of a cure? And why is there so much violence in the world that kills so many innocent people? The answer is simple: ignorance, fear, deception, and hate. And hate is the primary reason mankind can't find peace and security in the world. Hate is the reason the Jewish people have had to struggle so much and endure so much pain and misery.

All these things could be obliterated if only man could use the resources he has to wage war to rid the world of the misery it endures. Just think what it would be like if all those trillions of dollars used to build up military armies were used to feed and care for the world. Harmony would come to the world if people would only unite and build strong, good relationships with each other, and not hide anything, or lie to and deceive each other, and strive hard to understand we all have a right to live in this world. Loving one another instead of hating, and communicating daily to resolve problems before they get too large, could be a beginning.

If dictators were outlawed in all nations, and democracy were accepted as the only kind of government a country could have, and all the governments held dear the separation of church and state, the new glorious beginning would have begun. Eventually all nations will merge together and this world can eliminate all of its problems through communication and understanding, by finding the one element to unite us: love.

Until mankind can come to grips with himself and realize that we all have a right to be on this planet, the struggle for justice and equality will continue. No man should be looked down on and falsely judged for what he believes in, or how he looks, or what color his skin is, or where he is born, or how he believes in God. All men think and act differently, but we are all the same when it comes to belonging to the human race. God created us all. We all are God's creations.

Maybe this book will make the ignorant more intelligent and help the blind to see; then maybe the unjustified fears we all have in our minds will be replaced with compassion and understanding. But nothing will change this world until the hate people have growing in their hearts and minds is overcome. Overcoming the hate people have for the Jewish people will be the first step toward victory for all of mankind. And the Jewish people will be at the front of this endeavor. They will one day bring into being one who will capture Lucifer and enslave him for a thousand years. In this time mankind will have a thousand years of peace and prosperity. This book will activate this time, or at least I hope it will.

The real hate for the Jewish people came when Jesus was crucified. That is where I begin and end this chapter. That is when the Jewish people were deceived more than they were at any other time in their history. They were blamed for killing Jesus, so this is when all the people of the world started hating them.

When Jesus was alive, the Romans ruled and dominated the people of Judea with an iron hand. Their way was law, and anyone who didn't obey was arrested, imprisoned, or killed. The corrupt king Herod was under Rome's thumb. Anything they wanted they got through Herod.

The Roman influence didn't stop at the political realm but was also in the religious realm. The religious leaders of the day were all too helpful for the Romans. They knew they could be replaced at any moment, so they eagerly served their masters well.

The Romans were a different group of people. They came and conquered the land of Israel with the hardness of steel in their hearts and the power of destruction by their swords. Their legions were mighty and strong. Anyone who opposed them was easily defeated and destroyed. They ruled with a stern hand and controlled the entire region. They used their influence to corrupt the few so they could control the many. The religious leaders and the politicians of the day were all too eager to satisfy the Romans' demands. With their treachery and deceit, it would be safe to say they were the Devil's disciples.

It is here that the Jewish people were led astray. The Jewish religious leaders were so corrupt that even God couldn't unwind their tentacles of evil. The Devil has finally achieved a time and place to do his evil. He has set the stage to deceive the entire Jewish nation into turning against themselves to self-destruction.

The high priests and the Pharisees looked on the people like they were God. Their self-righteous ways gave them a sense of being special and having the right to judge and condemn all others. But all of them were nothing but pawns of the Roman authority. Their deceived minds thinking they were better than everyone else would lead to their demise. The Romans controlled them so well that they didn't know what was right or wrong. These men were the ones who judged and condemned the people. The Devil had his way by giving them a feeling of superiority when in fact they were only doing his bidding and the Romans provided the means.

After Jesus was crucified, the Devil wanted to erase everything about him from the world. He wanted the world to forget about who Jesus was and what he did. He used the Roman and Jewish leaders to implement this decree. But they all failed! The story of Jesus was preached throughout the world. His message of love and forgiveness changed the lives of all mankind. The world was saved by this Jewish carpenter in his suffering and dying for the sins of man.

This was a sad time for the Jewish people as a whole. The deception they were told warped their spiritual beliefs. They could not accept that one of their own was the Christ.

Only the Devil could conjure up this deception. He used the Jewish people as the scapegoats for all the ills of mankind. They were the tools he used to bring more hate into the world. This hate won over many souls he needed to overthrow the kingdom of God.

Hate brings violence, and violence brings death. The Jewish people now would be used to put hate into the hearts of mankind and turn that hate into death and wickedness.

I believe the main reason Jesus died on the cross was to save those souls who have committed sins. He knew that most sins are done because the one doing the sinning has been deceived into doing them. The pride in their hearts will not allow themselves to admit their wrongdoing. He sacrificed his life in this most horrific way so others would come to realize and admit to their wrongdoing. He died so all of mankind will be saved from eternal damnation. It was the way it had to be done. He suffered long and hard on that cross. If he had died any other way, it would have soon been forgotten. He suffered this agonizing way so people from all walks of life would see what love and forgiveness is all about. Jesus forgave those who crucified him when he was on that cross. That is what love and forgiveness is really all about.

The pride in mankind's heart prevents him from seeing the truth. Experiencing how Jesus died melts away that self-pride and shows that individual veracity. Whether you want to believe in Jesus Christ or not, he still died for the sins of all mankind. The ones before his birth, and the ones after his crucifixion, and the ones in between: he died so *all* of mankind would have their sins forgiven. It is just as plain as that!

Jesus willingly gave his life for the sins of mankind. He allowed himself to be sacrificed on the cross. No one should hate the Jewish people or anyone else for his death. It was Jesus' destiny to suffer and die. He decided his fate. He forgave those who crucified him while on the cross. But the Devil used this act to conjure up hate toward these simple people. The Jewish people had to bear the burden of having sent Jesus to the cross. Even though they were deceived in doing so, no matter: they had to suffer for their hateful decision to have Jesus crucified.

The world soon started hating the Jewish people with a more intense passion. They were looked on as a weak people who were consumed with religion. In time the Jewish people were blamed for all things, not just Jesus' death.

Only the Devil could devise a plan to turn people against one another by imposing hate toward the Jewish people for killing Jesus. This hate robbed men of their souls. The Devil's plan was in place. Get the world to kill, and exterminate the entire Jewish race so they will not bring into being the one who will bring an end to the Devil's domain in the world.

After Jesus was crucified, the Romans remained in Judea and maintained control of the Jewish people. In 66 AD an uprising resulted in Jerusalem being burned to the ground. This was the first but not the last time Jerusalem would be destroyed.

After the first century AD was over, the world was still controlled by those nations that used force and aggression to overpower and rule the meek.

Man became evil without any guidelines to control his natural aggression. Murder was not uncommon. Large armies were formed to attack and conquer simple, modest nations. Those who had the sword, and were willing to use it, became the masters of the world.

Christianity was growing, and the message of Jesus Christ was reaching people and changing their lives with a profound effect.

Most of the Jewish people rejected Jesus as the savior of the world, although some individuals believed in Jesus. In fact, the first Christians were Jewish. But as time went on, most of the Jewish people rejected Jesus and were persecuted for doing so. The Devil had put a mark on them as a race of people to be hated.

He needed souls, and the only way to get them was to trick and deceive man into sinning, with murder as the ultimate sin. Hate was the intoxicant used to warp the intellect to unleash the violence needed to inflict death. The evil forces of the world knew how to administer hate and to use it to get what they wanted.

As the centuries came and went, the hatred toward the Jewish people grew more and more intense; the Arabs hated them, and the self-righteous Christians hated them. Any group of people who would not admit the truth could now blame their faults and hardships on the Jewish people. Only the true Christians forgave them and accepted them for who they were.

The Jewish people have a certain look all to themselves. This look is just another way for prejudices to take hold. Anytime a group of people look different from all the others, it is easy to ridicule them. Looking different is no reason to make fun of someone. People find it easy to look down on others just because of their appearance.

Another thing: the Jewish people work hard in their own assembly. They strive for excellence. They struggle to make something of themselves and be successful in life. By working in a tightly knit group and supporting their race, they prosper. This is another reason people hate the Jewish people. They are jealous of their success. Those who are down on their luck and have nothing find it easy to feel sorry for themselves and hate those who have wealth. It is so with the Jewish people, for they are inspired to make something of their life, not just for themselves but also for God.

The Jewish people were hated for sending Jesus to the cross. Denying he was the Son of God and failing to acknowledge that Jesus died for the sins of the world only made it easier for the Devil to deceive mankind. He used the Jewish people to conjure up hate, and hate is the poison that turns men into monsters—monsters to devour the innocent and the meek.

CHAPTER 3

Lucifer's Two Arms of Power

EVER SINCE THE BEGINNING of time, the Devil has been obsessed with taking over the world and using man to do it for him. His determination has been profound and ruthless over the ages. He is determined to rule the world so God will have no dominion over any part of it. He has deceived mankind time and time again. His lure of lust and power has led many a man and woman to do his evil works in an attempt to enslave mankind.

He has used force to control nations. The Romans took over most of the world and controlled it very effectively for many hundreds of years, but they couldn't maintain control. Probably the main reasons they failed were that they fought among themselves and did not have a government that was strong enough and smart enough to keep control of the lands they conquered. They were known as the First Reich all the way up to Napoleon's time.

Many nations and many a dictator engaged in war to take land only temporarily until they were thrown out. To rule the world one must have a plan to maintain control. One must win over the hearts and minds of the people so rebellion can be eliminated, or at least easy enough to put down.

To take land by force and enslave its inhabitants one must be vicious and cruel. Having an army big enough to overwhelm its victims is mandatory. Then once a nation is conquered, there must be put into place an order to maintain control.

The Romans maintained their control by empowering stooge leaders and giving them power over their people. They were traitors to their people, but as long as they had this power and authority, they did what the Romans wanted. In turn they kept the peace while Rome continued with its conquests. This worked for a while until the people realized that their leaders were traitors, and then they organized to rebel against them.

For the Devil to control the world he needed a plan to prevent rebellion. To maintain control of the entire world one must have a political theory to enslave the mind and heart, not just the physical body of mankind. He needed an organization that could seduce the people and then take away their will. What he needed was a political theory to be implemented and accepted by the people as a new way of life—a theory that could control the masses long enough so the government could intervene and prevent any rebellion. This is what the Devil needs to take over the world.

The world is too big for one man to invade lands and conquer them all. By the time he has finished one conquest, another one of his past conquests begins to rebel and unravel. No, the world is just too big for one man to conquer it all with force as his only instrument. There needs to be put in place a seductive element imposed on the people fixing to be conquered, so that their will to be free is neutralized. That is the main reason the Devil hasn't achieved his main objective. He hasn't found that seductive element of control yet—or has he?

People have always treasured their freedom. It is in the DNA that makes us human: to be free to think as we like, to believe in God the way we want, to live the way we want. Right or wrong, good or bad, as long as we have the freedom to live life as we choose, that is what is important and what makes us who we are. This desire to be free is embedded in the soul of all mankind.

Those who want to take away that freedom are doing the Devil's work. He doesn't want us to be free. He wants us to be enslaved and controlled by his legions of evil and forced to obey his doctrine and only his doctrine. Then God will have to destroy the world.

One must understand that there are things going on in this world that can't be explained. There are forces in the world that are forging the Devil's plans right now, and there are forces in the world forging God's plan that we can't see. Sometimes they collide and cause havoc, but rest assured that God's plan will win in the long run.

There may be a lot suffering that has to be imposed on people to achieve this, but the self-sacrifices and misery that must be felt, in God's eyes, will not go unrecognized. The ones who endure this suffering will be rewarded someday.

One must have faith that God is right and He knows what He is doing. God is always right! Don't ever forget that. It is man who is fallible. It is man who blames God for his short comings. And religion can be the substance to easily warp the minds of man when hate and deception are added. Man is full of sin; God isn't.

For the Devil to achieve his goal of controlling the world, he must learn how to trick man into surrendering his will to him. He must know what pleasure to addict him to, to put lust into his heart so truth can be blocked. Showing him the things of this world will be more important than his afterlife. For the Devil to rule the world, he must overcome the masses with an intoxicant to enslave their minds and hearts if he is to consume their souls.

The Devil will have to master two major forces to achieve the goal of world domination. They should be called the left and right arms of the Devil: the two institutions of power to confuse and divide the people of this planet. Those two forces are politics and religion.

These two forces are greatly habituated by the masses. They reach deep into one's mind, heart, and soul like nothing else. If used right they can benefit mankind tremendously, but if used wrong they can lead to a path of corruption and evil. The power they offer can overcome the spirit and bring temptation and turn a good man into a bad one.

The vast amounts of money these two institutions have can control people, and once they are controlled, the Devil can use these individuals to deceive the masses they lead to do his bidding; having access to large amounts of money is the key to obtaining power.

The power and the prestige these institutions offer are sometimes acquired by unorthodox means. When this happens, the journey to the top may be maintained only by covering up the past and doing things terribly wrong. And those who have reached the top may not want to relinquish their power. The sins of the past may then be exposed. Covering up wrongdoing can lead to evil acts all the way up to murder.

The Devil's right arm is the power of religion. This is how he reaches out and takes control of mankind more effectively than any other way. This right arm is his most powerful strength and mankind's biggest weakness. When someone thinks he is doing God's will when he isn't, it is hard to change that person's mind and tell him differently. The power of religion is a force that is forged by the beliefs that are in the soul. And when the belief is wrong, the Devil can easily control the outcome.

Religion is a way people can worship God and feel like in the end they will go to heaven when they die. I guess that is the main reason people believe in God. This concept has compelled many to live a life full of false thoughts. God didn't put us on this planet just to die and go to heaven. He put us on this planet to live and feel the wonderful feelings of life, to love and care for one another, to feel life and experience all that life has to offer. As long as we live, God is real!

Because religion was made by man, it is also controlled by man. Church leaders, and there are many, have power over individuals like no one else. They represent what God wants us to believe. Religion can also be controlled by the Devil when the leaders of these churches are led astray and get caught up with the ways of the world. When one religion clashes with a different one, then war, violence, and death come, and God is caught in the middle.

There is no such thing as one perfect religion. I think if there was only one religion in the world, the Devil could and would somehow control it and then mankind would be doomed. There must be different beliefs in God so mankind won't be so easily deceived, then controlled, and then perish.

I will not name all the religions there are and start telling about all their negative things or hang-ups. I will be respectful to all religions out there, and I mean all.

Respect for others and how they believe is something all people who love God should practice. Just because someone thinks differently or worships God differently or feels differently about things doesn't mean I should hate or dislike that person. We all have a right to be ourselves and think differently. Respect for others is something all of mankind should try to do. The world is a big place and full of different cultures and beliefs.

My personal belief is in Jesus Christ. My belief in God is through Jesus. I think that the purpose of the horrible suffering and death Jesus went through was to save mankind by dying for our sins. But if there were only one religion, Christianity, the Devil would find a way to manipulate it and use it to deceive mankind to destroy itself.

Look at what many Christians did to the Jewish people all throughout history: forcing them to repent of their sins, killing and murdering them for crucifying Christ, and blaming them for all the other ills mankind has gone through. The Jewish people were the perfect scapegoats for all of man's hardships. And it was the Christian groups that did most of the persecuting.

Just look at what the conquistadors did. In the name of Jesus they enslaved the Aztec Indians and murdered tens of thousands of them.

When the slave traders enslaved men and women from Africa and brought them to America, they used Christianity as a reason for their enslaving practices. Bringing Jesus up made their wicked ways easier. They thought they were doing the Africans a favor by bringing Christianity into their lives.

Wherever there is a religion that makes people feel superior and right with God, the Devil will be close by to warp that belief and use that person or people to do his will.

Let's get this straight. The present-day Jewish community did not crucify Jesus, so they should not be persecuted for sending him to the cross. Next, Jesus willingly decided to die for the sins of mankind. He willingly gave his life. If Jesus hadn't died on the cross, nobody would know anything about him. The sins of man would not have been washed away by his blood. It was this action of being nailed to a cross that made Jesus who he is. He had to die this way if mankind was to be saved. It was Jesus' decision to die this way, so no group of people should be persecuted for what Jesus did. Even when he was suffering on that cross, he asked God to forgive them for they knew not what they were doing. If Jesus can forgive those who crucified him, why can't all men do the same?

Jesus Christ isn't a religion anyway. He was a man whose actions, not just words, defined who and what he was and did for all of mankind.

When two people come together who believe in Jesus and have different views about how they should believe in him, it becomes a religion.

Not all Christians think, act, or believe the same. They all feel differently about things in life and about Jesus.

There is so much terrorism in the world, and the ones doing the violence feel like they are doing God's will. They are led by men who feel strongly that their belief in God is the only belief that should be in the world. They think they have the right to murder innocent people, and use God as their justification. The power of religion gives them that feeling.

I could go on and on about how religion can warp and confuse people into doing things that are wrong. I will leave this part now. Just be on the alert and do not let this element, this arm of the Devil, capture and keep you in his grip. Religion is intended to bring people closer to God, not warp their intelligence and push them apart, thereby doing the Devil's work.

The left arm of the Devil is just as powerful as the right but not as easily manipulated. It is the arm of the Devil that has power over the people's minds instead of their hearts. It works through ideology or credo, the way a person thinks and feels without a certain belief in God. The left arm of the Devil is politics.

Politics brings together people in a most magnetic but diverse way. When people think the same way, politics is the forum that unites them. This institution can be used for good, but also for bad. When people who think the same come together and form parties, each political party is a theology of how these people believe and live their lives. It is a union to shape values and understand how someone thinks without truly knowing them. The political party you belong to tells the world how you think about numerous things, although it does not allow people to actually know you. Politics is broken down into parties. And the party you belong to is like the religion you belong to, except it isn't God that is the center of attraction, it is everything else—and I mean everything else.

Politics is compelling and interesting to all human beings in some ways. Even at a young age, belonging to a political party shapes the way you think and believe and act, and gives you a place of belonging. It also gives a young person the initiative to think about important topics and shapes who they are and what they believe in. Doing this develops a person into someone with a strong character and gives them a purpose in life. But sometimes that purpose can be warped and altered to do evil. That is why I call it the Devil's left arm.

Political power like religious power is created by money. Money is the substance that makes the world turn, not just in politics but in religious matters too. The churches of the world would not have the power they have without the money people give them. In politics people give money so they can be a part of something bigger than themselves. The other way to raise money is by way of taxes.

If you can make people pay a third or half of what they make, the political people who control this money can achieve power on a level that is hard to conceive or comprehend. And when you have people who have access to large amounts of money, they can do good things or they can do horrible things with these funds.

Like I said earlier, money is the substance that makes the world turn. It can be used to feed the hungry or it can be used to kill the innocent. Those who have control over this money have power, and these two institutions (religion and politics) are where the money is most abundant. The Devil knows he must control the people who have the most money if he is to rule the world.

He doesn't have to control all the money. He knows evil can be implemented even by using small amounts, as long as the money is used as a tool to deceive. He puts money into the hands of those who are eager to do evil. That is why there is so much wickedness in the world. Men who control vast amounts of cash can use it to deceive the poor into doing evil. Those who have lots of money should be watched carefully so their actions can be monitored before they cross over the line and become disciples of the Devil.

For the Devil to rule the world, he must create a religion and a political party that will be appealing to the majority, and then blend these two groups into one. If he can persuade people to join an organization that brings together his left and right arms, he will begin to set the stage to one day take over the world. This must not happen! This must not take place! I write this chapter to prevent the evil forces from organizing or bringing to pass this one-state-of-mind way of thinking.

Politics should remain in the arena where political matters are discussed. Religion should remain in the church. The separation of church and state should always be recognized and accepted.

When religious matters are consumed by politics and political matters are warped with religious beliefs, you will have nothing but chaos!

That is why the Middle East has so much violence and is in such disarray. Religious groups control the political spectrum. And as long as they do, the other religious groups who don't agree with the ones in power will always have hatred in their hearts. There will always be hatred and violence where church and state are forged into a single government and dictate one way of thinking. It is essential to separate these two groups and make sure they don't take away any freedoms. People should be able to live without being controlled through intimidation.

When a Democrat who is a Christian and a Republican who is also a Christian can disagree on political matters, then you have a good balance. But when someone belongs to a certain religious group but doesn't belong to any political party, there won't be a balance, because anyone who doesn't belong to that religion will be alienated and pushed away from political matters. There will be no balance.

People who belong to the same religion don't necessarily get along and agree on everything. If a Muslim who does not belong to any political party dictates what should be done politically, then all others will have to agree with him or become alienated. This will cause an unbalance.

When a government has control of all the money that is raised to run itself and is ruled by one religious leader, or one religious group, then all the people of that country have to belong to this one religion or be pushed aside and ignored. They in turn will be either controlled by that government or not heard.

If the people don't have a say about how things are run, then the people of that country have been enslaved. For a country to have a legitimate government, it must subscribe to the institution of democracy. Any government that is not of the people, for the people, and by the people is a government of evil. No government should be run by one leader, or one religious group, or one political party. For a government to function properly, there must be a balance. And to obtain that balance there must be a separation of church and state.

The people who make up a country should be the ones who vote and elect their leaders. And those elected officials should be innovative and given the ability to decide what is best for their people. There needs to be an understanding that they are responsible for their future. They need to be able to disagree without killing one another and to understand that all people think differently. These leaders should have respect for others who do not think the same, or worship the same, or believe the same. We are all individuals and should be looked at as individuals. The future shouldn't be controlled by some dictator but by the will of the people.

All Muslims don't think the same. All Christians don't think the same. All Jewish people don't think the same. All Democrats don't think the same. All Republicans don't think the same. Well, most do, but not all. Well, maybe. You get the idea. All people have different views on political matters as well as religious matters.

The leaders of governments should govern with the concept of how their children will be better off. They should treat all people with the same compassion and understanding regardless of what religion they belong to, and strive for a better tomorrow for the next generation. There must be a balance of political theory and religious beliefs and no attempt to forge the two into one. They must remain separate!

Until the governments of the Middle East are governed by political parties and not religious groups, there will always be conflicts in that region. Politics and religion are very important to the people of this world. They both serve the masses as ways to bring harmony to the world and in turn make the world a better place to live. But when you try to blend political ideas with one religious idea, the Devil will be there to nurture this idea and try to deceive man again.

As long as the Devil's right and left arms are separated, mankind has a chance to defeat him. But while the Devil can use people in religion and politics, he has a chance to take over the world. It is only the people, in their large masses, who will be able to prevent him from achieving this endeavor. The people of this world should never be enslaved. The determination to remain free is the intangible substance that keeps the

Devil from ever ruling this world. The people should always have the freedom of speech, the freedom of religion, and the freedom to think as individuals. As long as they do, the world will live and grow as God intended.

CHAPTER 4

The Coming of the Antichrist (The Prince of Evil)

HE HAS COME AND he has gone, this terrible man of hate—a man of revenge, murder, and destruction. He is dead now. Mankind can live easier now that the Antichrist is dead. This man was born in a time when his evil could do the most harm. He was born into this world like any other boy from a normal town, a boy looking for his identity who was abused badly by his father. He in turn abused the world with a viciousness of demon like proportion. A theory of a master race was the inspiration to crush the world into submission, ending with the "Final Solution" to the Jewish question. What to do with the Jewish people?

His mother bore him when she was twenty-eight years old. He was like any other boy born into this world. He was raised in a time of peace in a small country in Europe. He learned from the past and paved the way for a new horrific future for the world. He did so with war and destruction never seen before. He developed a hatred for the Jewish people that could be conjured up only from the bowels of hell. The Devil gave him praise like no other before him. He was born on April 20, 1889. His name was Adolf Hitler.

Before this man could become the Antichrist, the world had to be formed and constructed a certain way for him to be most effective when he unleashed his wickedness. It was like mankind prepared the world for his coming. First, a history of militarism and violence had to be laid down for him to build on, with nations turning against one another in a violent struggle between free and slave.

It was a time before man could seek out peaceful ways to live and grow, before technology could make it easier to communicate better. Time was running out for the Devil to rule the world. He had only one more chance to try to conquer the world by force, to empower one who could smash the world into submission. The world was set; the time was right to bring into the world the spirit of the Antichrist.

God had his son come into the world, so the Devil would have his. He was born in the nineteenth century. He evolved in the twentieth century as the one to do the Devil's work like no other before him: to put into action the overall plan Satan had for 5,000 years, to conquer the world and destroy the entire Jewish race—all of them. It was time to round up all the Jewish people from every corner of the world and kill them. He knew the Jewish people would one day create a messiah, a savior to rid the world of evil and reign in a thousand years of peace, a peace for all of God's children.

Before the Antichrist could execute his evil plans, the world had to be set. The political and religious groups of the world had to be in tune for his coming.

The time is January 1933. The Devil with a mischievous grin waves his scepter over Europe. The environment and economic situation are perfect. The economies of the world are in their worst shape ever. When large masses of unemployed people are flooding the planet and food is hard to come by, the soil becomes rich and fertile to sow the seeds of evil, including, of course, blaming the Jewish community for these unfortunate times. Anti-Semitism is echoed throughout the land. People need to blame somebody for their misery and hardships, and the Jewish people are once again playing that role.

Who is this man, Adolf Hitler? Why did he come to Germany to be the leader of this country? He was born in Austria the third child of Klara and Alois Hitler.

I believe that when someone is born into this world, God already has a plan for what that person will become. I think the Devil has a plan already set up too.

Some people are just born to do evil, once evil has entered their heart. Evil enters a man's heart through his eyes and then intoxicates the spirit with worldly desires, and then those desires become lusty and dynamic. Soon the lusts overcome the person and the evil grows until it devours the soul.

There are three steps the Devil takes to win over a man's soul: the temptations of the eye, the lust of the flesh, and the pride of life. He doesn't do it any other way.

The environment plays a large role in how much evil one can do. When a person succumbs to the ways of the world, hate, revenge, lust for power, having authority, attaining the authority, the past, the future—all these things contribute to how much evil one will perform.

The world moves in directions. When you have someone caught up with the ways of the world, he or she tries to change the world. In their minds they may have good intentions, but the road they journey down can be warped with thoughts of hate and in turn twist good intentions until monsters are created.

One must never be obsessed with changing the world too quickly. Do what you feel is right and be on the lookout for the deceptions of this world and try not to let them trick you. Do only what is in your control. If the world is to change, it will on its own. It takes only one man or one woman to ignite the spark of change; the masses will do the rest by keeping the flame glowing.

On TV I see people killing one another in the Middle East and surrounding countries. Shooting guns, throwing rocks, chanting hateful rhetoric, all kinds of malicious acts, suicide bombers blowing themselves up just to kill others—this madness will never be accepted in God's eyes. These individuals are delusional about doing God's work. The many distortions in the minds of these individuals are outrageous. The ones doing this are also victims. They throw away their lives because someone convinced them they are doing God's work. These individuals have gotten caught up with the ways of the world.

Some people who live in a poor environment and feel the misery of hunger and are without basic human needs are eager to die and end their miserable existence. God would be ashamed of these people who take away innocent life. Life is too precious to throw away, but to take away someone else's life because you are mad at the world is wrong. Those suicide bombers and those who trick them into becoming one will feel God's wrath one day. You can be sure they will never enter the kingdom of heaven, no matter what good intentions they have or religious group they belong to. When God shows them what they have done, the shame of their actions will burn like fire!

There was another that got caught up with the ways of the world. He also was brought up in a poor environment. He also was eager to take away innocent life.

The trickery Adolf Hitler practiced was compounded with his passion as a speaker. He used patriotism to warp the minds of the people in Germany. He blamed the Jewish people for Germany's defeat in World War I and everything else. When people hear what they want to hear, it moves them in a direction away from the truth. And that is just what Hitler did to the German people. The German people were the perfect audience for Hitler's speeches and in a perfect place to be led away from the truth.

Germany was at fault for starting World War I by invading a neutral country, Belgium. Germany divided its armies into two parts; by doing so it could never decisively win at either end. They chose to fight a war on two fronts, with Russia in the east and France in the west. It was Germany's aggressive actions that started the war in the first place. After losing the war, the people of Germany didn't want to hear the truth.

Adolf Hitler made sure they didn't. Revenge was the burning acid that consumed his soul. Hitler couldn't admit that Germany had lost the war. He blamed the ones who brought the peace. His hatred grew out of the lies he told himself. He blamed others for Germany's demise. He sought revenge and brought about destruction to all of Germany. His proud heart couldn't accept the truth that Germany was at fault for the war.

The seeds of deceptions were planted in his mind and fertilized by lies and more lies, cultivated by the burning desire for revenge in his proud heart, which brought forth the harvest of death for the people of Germany and the world.

Patriotism is deeply revered in the hearts and minds of a proud people. To admit they were wrong, or to admit that their government was wrong in fighting and losing this war, was something the German people couldn't and wouldn't accept. The compelling lies and deceptive stories they read in the newspapers telling them of victory after victory and then sudden defeat was more than the German people could comprehend. These lies set the stage to beguile the masses of Germany.

This gave Hitler the opportunity to rise to power by telling the German people just what they wanted to hear. He blamed the Jewish race without any truth to back it up. He then used democracy to get elected, after which he destroyed democracy to prevent any others from taking over the government.

Every man wants to feel important. Every man wants to feel important and have his life be of consequence. Achieving power is how many men get this feeling. To feel power is to experience utopia in the light of the real world. To feel in charge and to lead the masses toward something you want done is a passion for some men.

This is what Adolf Hitler wanted, and once there, he didn't want to relinquish this power. He didn't want to lay down the scepter of authority. He started to lie and cheat and murder to stay in power. Once he had done that, staying in power meant preventing anyone from knowing what evil he had done. As long as you call the shots, no one will know, but when you don't have power anymore, you become a victim of your past.

Because of one's pride, one doesn't want to expose the bad things one has done, so one has to do more evil to continue to cover up the past. That is why dictators should never be allowed to stay in power. No one should be above the law, and when one is, the laws are tossed out the window. Then more and more evil will eventually take place.

When someone is born into the world, he or she is without sin. One must commit many sins before one can graduate to a level of horrendous sins. One sin leads to other sin, then another, then another, and so on. This continues until sin becomes easy and done without thought. It is the continuing nature of sin that makes men into monsters. And with more power or influence, someone can elevate the sin into gargantuan size.

People in high places have a greater responsibility to live right and be accountable for their actions. When they have the power to cover up things by lying and deceiving, more bad things will happen.

If the German people had been told the truth during World War I and afterward, it would have been harder for Hitler to seduce and lead Germany into another world war.

The past played a big part in how and why Adolf Hitler became the ruthless tyrant he was. The history of Germany is filled with militarism, violence, and war making.

When a people have a history of militarism and war making, it is only logical that one will arise and want to do these things again. One must not idolize evil men. Schools should teach children realistic history and then make clear who the evil men are. When people suffer in times of war, one must not admire the ones who inflicted the suffering. They should be told of everything that happens, not just the things that sound great, and plainly define the good and the evil.

When the youth of Germany were idolizing Hitler, they were in turn surrendering their souls for what he believed in. Those taught in early years are more easily controlled later in life. Truth is the only thing that can break the chains of deception.

When those who hate someone teach that hate to a young person, that young person will grow up and perpetrate that hate he has learned. God will punish those who teach hate. Hate is the virus that will lead to damnation. If one hates someone, this virus will lead to one's own destruction. The hate Hitler had for the Jewish people eventually steered him to his own demise.

He invaded country after country just to gather up the Jewish people so he could kill them. He was a destroyer of the Jewish race and by doing so destroyed the lives of the people who loved him more than anything: the German people. The most disturbing thing about Hitler's hate for the Jewish people is it was all a lie he had in his mind.

I guess the reason Hitler turned out to be a monster was that he had the ability to alter the truth. He had in him the ability to hate like no one else. He would lie to himself just so he could hate more. It was like he was on a drug—a drug his mind conjured up when he started to hate. This drug became an addiction so that when he needed a fix, he would trick himself by lying more about the Jewish people. The lies he told himself produced more and more of this drug. I think this hate substance flowing in his mind, along with all the other drugs he was on, amplified his passions and created the emotional speaker he was famous for being.

It is hard to imagine that our brains are constantly creating different chemical compounds every day, but they are.

When hate is thought in the brain, a chemical does get created. But why would someone continue to think hateful thoughts and experience this feeling? I don't believe the individual knows what is going on. I believe false thoughts bring on this sensation. Adolf Hitler constantly lied to himself. These lies he told himself, or voices, made up false cerebrations that produced the chemical of his addiction. These hateful thoughts overwhelmed his ability to think straight, and what resulted was the Holocaust.

All people hate. Hate is something that comes naturally. If you think long enough, hate will enter your mind. And if you do it enough, the chemical that causes hate can become addictive. There are two types of hateful thoughts: true hate and false hate.

True hate is something real. If someone walks up to you with vengeance in their eyes and says you're as fat as a cow, you will feel hurt and take offense and hate that person. This is real hate, because what happened is real. The words came out of someone's mouth and were actually spoken directly to you. You heard a real person's voice and took offense and started to hate that person. If someone walks up to you and slaps you in the face, you react with anger and then with hate. If people didn't have the ability to hate, you wouldn't be able to take up for yourself and would eventually die. So hate is a normal emotion if it is real. But what if it isn't real?

Say someone walks up to you and comments that you look like you've gained a few pounds. They don't mean any harm; it was just a thoughtless comment, and the person walks away. Then you start to think. You begin to lie to yourself and hear that person say other bad things about you. In fact they didn't, but you manufacture these false thoughts about this person and begin to hate this person. This is false hate—something that never happened but you tell yourself it did.

It is like hearing voices of your mother or father telling you something that really bothers you, or them asking questions you have answered before and now it bothers you when they continue to ask them, or when they criticize you for something and it really makes you mad. They don't say these things, but your mind tells you they did, and then you begin to hate them. This is where the addiction takes hold. When you lie to yourself, or manufacture false voices of people who are close to you by having them say something that really gets under your skin, then you begin to hate. This hate, this chemical compound, will continue to circulate through your mind as long as you think these thoughts.

The longer you hate, the longer you are experiencing this chemical compound. Then you start to believe that these false hateful thoughts are real. You take action to rid yourself of these people, thinking that will rid you of the hate. It doesn't. It only makes you more susceptible to the substance and the substance is hate.

When Hitler made negative statements about the Jewish people, they all were false. Not once did the statements have any veracity.

His belief in the so-called master race theology or feeling better than any other race of people gave him a false sense of superiority as a human being. The idea that he may have had Jewish blood in his veins gave him another reason to falsely hate the Jewish people. It's hard to feel superior when you know you might have Jewish ancestry in your family tree.

There was a war going on in Hitler's mind: the battle to rid himself of his Jewish ancestry, to rid himself of the Jewish blood flowing in his veins. His determination to rid Germany of the Jewish people was an attempt to rid himself of this element. This brought on lies on top of the lies he was telling himself. His whole life was a lie, and he tried to make it true.

On January 30, 1933, Adolf Hitler became chancellor of Germany. This was the start of the Holocaust. This was the beginning of the worst time mankind has ever experienced. This is where Adolf Hitler was given the power to do his evil. This is the day when Hitler became the Antichrist.

He became the leader of the Third Reich. The First Reich was the Holy Roman Empire; it started with Julius Caesar and lasted right up until Napoleon's time. Then the Second Reich began with Kaiser Wilhelm I in 1871 and lasted until the Russian Revolution of 1917.

In 1933 the economies of the world were in shambles. Tens of millions of people were unemployed, and the world was in a perfect state for evil to flourish. At no other time had the world been in such terrible shape.

The Great Depression was in its fourth year. People were not ready to combat what lay ahead. A mad man with a funny mustache and the dream to smash the world into submission had come into power. He just needed time to rearm Germany's military, and he did it. He did this in secret so the world would not see what he was up to.

From 1933 to 1939, the Devil molded Hitler into the man he wanted him to become: a man to do his evil and execute his plan to exterminate all the Jewish people in Europe, then later on the whole world.

There are seven deadly sins of emotions to destroy one's self. These things by themselves are not sins. They are emotions. But when these emotions are not controlled, they can become sins. These deadly sins of emotions are the essential elements to turn one's heart against God. And left unchecked they can devour a person's soul before one realizes it. It takes only one of these sins of emotions to alter the character to change a person to destroy one's self.

We all are human, and we all must learn to control our emotions. We must maintain and stay in control of our feelings and passions. Once we lose control, it is nearly impossible to live right and to be good. Men who are weak in spirit and do not eagerly struggle to stay in control of themselves are subjected to losing their soul and living an empty life without God. To understand more about these sins of emotions, here is the list of what they are.

The Seven Deadly Sins of Emotions
    1. Anger
    2. Hate
    3. Lust
    4. Envy
    5. Glutton
    6. Greed
    7. Pride

Remember, these are not sins by themselves. They become sins when we lose control of them. Every man, woman, and child on this planet has these emotions in them. They make up our personhood. It is the lack of control of these emotions that ruins our lives.

Now back to Hitler.

It is still January 1933. The Devil has six years to mold Hitler, and he will use these seven traits to alter his normal human character. This will be the time to re-create him into a semi-God-like monster that will try to conquer the world and exterminate the entire Jewish race.

First is anger. After World War I was over, the truth of losing it was made known to the German people. A humiliating defeat to a proud people was something the German people just couldn't accept, and Hitler was no exception.

It was all the lies the German government told while the war was going on that warped the minds of the people. They were told of victory after victory when in fact the victories were horrible defeats. The German army in the latter stages of the Great War was nearly ready to capitulate.

The beginning of the war was honorable. Germany came to the defense of Austria-Hungary when Russia took up for Serbia. But when the Germans invaded Belgium to get at France, they were looked upon as the aggressor, and they were. The world blamed Germany for escalating the war.

When the people of Germany were told after the war that they had to pay reparations for the war, they couldn't understand why. Kaiser Wilhelm had run off to Holland because he was afraid of being imprisoned. If he had been arrested and tried, the people would have known the truth and wouldn't have been so naïve about what went on after the war. But he wasn't, and the German people easily accepted the lies they were fed. This deception amplified the anger and made it easier for Hitler to make his move and seduce a nation into surrendering it to him.

Hitler's speeches were full of anger about why Germany lost the Great War and gave him the opportunity to poison the minds of the German people. Hitler was polluted with anger. This emotion became not just a sin but a wicked sin that led to another: hate.

Hate and anger are different. When you feel angry, you are mad at things in general, but when you have hate in your mind, it is concentrated on a single thing. In this case it was the Jewish people. Hitler blamed the end of the Great War on the signing of the Armistice by the social democrats and the Jews.

Also, his hatred for the Jewish people went way back in his life. The Jewish people looked different from regular Germans. There has always been bias toward the appearance of people who look different. Anyone who looks odd or dissimilar is subjected to ridicule and later on, hate.

Maybe it wasn't just looks but jealousy.

The Jewish people worked together like no other group of people in history; by working together in a tight-knit group, they prospered tremendously.

There were some who didn't because of the times.

When you have the support of family and others in your faith, success is more easily reached. At this most difficult for all people living in Germany seeing some prosper while others were starving made it easier to dislike the ones who were better off. This environment soon turned anger into hate. Misery can conjure up resentment very easily.

But Hitler's bloodlines were probably the main reason he hated the Jewish people. He felt he was poisoned by the Jewish blood running through his veins. Hitler's father was said to be the illegitimate son of a Jewish man. If this is so, and it probably is, Hitler's grandfather was Jewish, making Hitler one quarter Jewish. This thought of being part Jewish corrupted Hitler's thoughts and bloated his heart with a hatred that consumed his soul. It made him mad. It made him evil. It made him into something inhuman. It turned him into the Antichrist. It was this sin more than any other that transformed a regular man into a monster of mass murder. Hate is what caused Hitler to metamorphose into this diabolical, monstrous devil. He was totally absorbed with hate and by feeding his hate with more lies. He in turn instigated and brought about the Holocaust because of his inability to control his hate.

He thought if he could kill all the Jewish people, it would remove the Jewish elements in his body. How stupid this is! Ignorant thoughts about false things make the hate in one's own mind cultivate stupidity. Then the stupidity brings about something more terrible: violence and murder. There is nothing more terrible than ignorance in action.

I won't go on about why Hitler hated the Jewish people. Everyone knows his hatred for them was sinister and evil. He absorbed the sin of hate instead of rebelling against it.

One's heart and mind can easily absorb sin like a sponge, especially hate. It can then grow into an addiction like any other substance with habit-forming elements. It tricks the mind into using violence to "make right" the situation.

People who kill others because they hate them think they will rid themselves of the hatred by doing this horrible act. This is just plain stupid! Hate is plain stupid. It robs individuals of intelligence and what is real. It warps their other thoughts to make them evil and ready to do the Devil's work. Hate is against all that God is. And those who hate, and do the Devil's work in the name of God, are destined to never enter the kingdom of heaven—ever!

Sin is the self-inflicted shameful act that destroys one's inner self and prevents one from being close to God. God doesn't want us to sin, because he doesn't want us to suffer the shame the sin will cause and to continue doing something wrong. One must resist sin and not allow it to grow. It must be resisted no matter how hard it is to do. If you fail, then you will be the one to suffer.

Now it's time to get back to the third deadly sin of emotion: lust.

Hitler was also consumed by lust. When people hear the word *lust,* they automatically think of sex. In most cases, that is true, but it isn't always. Lust can be a sin of just wanting something a whole lot—an uncontrollable desire to have something. This overpowering thing consumes the heart, not just the physical parts of the body. It is the physical pleasures that overwhelm the senses and make you a slave to enjoying their inclinations. You can lust after anything that gives you pleasure physically or emotionally. In Hitler's case, he lusted for power.

The lust he had for obtaining and keeping power is viewed as sinister and complete. His lusty ambitiousness to obtain power overwhelmed all other things in his life. He wanted to take over the government and seize control of everything, and I mean everything: the government, the people, the church, the military, and everything else in Germany. He was consumed by the lust for power, and it was this lust that led to murder and every other sin in the book. The lust for power was Hitler's passion.

The next sin of emotion is envy. Yes, Hitler was envious of the Jewish people and what they had. When Hitler was trying to find himself before the Great War, he was poor. All people who were poor had great feelings of envy for people who had an abundance of things. The Jewish people in most cities, not all, had more than the average citizen. It is only normal to want things others have.

In Hitler's case envy for what the Jewish people had wasn't the only reason; he was envious of what God had. He wanted the worship that people had for God. He wanted to be worshipped. He wanted to be the only one to be worshipped. Since people were still worshipping God like they should, Hitler's envy put a stop to worshipping God. He had the churches destroyed. He had the clergy imprisoned and put in concentration camps. He outlawed God. His envy reached a height greater than the mountains in Asia. He wanted to be worshipped like a god. In his mind he was God.

This is what envy will do if left unchecked. It can turn a regular, honest man into a lying, cheating thief. Wanting things that others have can alter a man's thinking to the point where trickery and chicanery become an obsession. Envy will make a man steal or take things that aren't his. Envy will break down a man's character and lead him to a host of other sins. Envy is in all of us. It just needs to be controlled.

When Hitler came to power in January 1933, the Devil was with him. He worked with him and gave him the direction to start seeking revenge. To do this he needed to build up his military so that later he would have the means to use force to conquer countries and impose his will on them. He wanted to take everything. He wanted to conquer the world. The Devil poisoned his mind with greed. This is the fifth sin of emotion.

Greed is the intense desire for possessions and wealth. Greed had to be implanted into Hitler's mind so he would devour the world and do as much destruction as possible. He would not be satisfied with just Europe but wanted to take over the world. This has to be the ultimate greedy act: to conquer the world, to have everything, to have it to rule, and to make all the people in the world fall to their knees and worship him or die. Thank God this didn't come to pass. But it was greed that led Hitler into this expedition toward world conquest.

The next sin of emotion on the list is gluttony. I guess most people think gluttony is an uncontrollable act of eating food, just like lust is looked upon as a sin of the flesh. But gluttony is not just an overconsumption of food. It can be something else. Funk & Wagnalls dictionary says that a glutton is "one who has a great appetite or capacity for something"—a great appetite for something.

I guess Hitler was the most gluttonous person who has ever lived. He wasn't a glutton for food. No, he was a glutton for something more hideous and monstrous. He was a glutton for murder and death.

It was this sin of emotion that the Devil had to initiate into Hitler's mind to carry out his ultimate goal: the complete annihilation of the Jewish race. It was this sin of emotion the Devil conceived for Hitler so he would truly become the Antichrist.

Gluttony refers to an overwhelming appetite that can't be satisfied. Hitler's great appetite was for killing people! His main objective in his life was to consume the entire Jewish race and murder them all. This was his passion. This was his ultimate goal. He thought it was his destiny to kill every Jewish man, woman, and child on the face of the earth. This gluttonous endeavor was branded on his soul. Murder of the Jewish people was his feast. His thirst for murder was unquenchable! His taste for killing consumed millions and millions of innocent people's lives. His gluttonous desire for murder will never leave the memory of mankind. His insane passion to murder all the Jewish people in the world will never be forgotten as long as mankind is on this planet.

Those who choose not to believe or accept what Hitler did just show that there are people in the world who refuse to see or accept the truth. Those individuals who deny that the Holocaust ever took place are blinded by the hate that shields their conscience. God should shield His eyes from these individuals when they ask to enter His kingdom.

The last sin of emotion on the list is pride. Oh yes, pride. This is the primary sin that has destroyed the souls of many men throughout history, not just Hitler's. It is this sin of emotion that gave Hitler the inner strength and passion that eventually led to his destruction.

Pride: An undue sense on one's own superiority. That is a very good, concise definition of pride. A man can't live without pride. He must feel good about his actions and thoughts or he will be nothing. He would be a worthless, valueless, drossy human being without it. Pride is the substance that makes a man total and complete. It is the element that holds together his self-worth and self-determination and makes a person whole.

It brings about values that are right and good, and is the essential component that motivates and creates the ambition to become distinguished and noble. Without it a man would succumb to a meaningless life of emptiness, blankness, and vacuousness.

The emotion of pride also has its downfalls. It can lead to sin. Oh yes, it can lead a man down a path of total destruction. Many a man's soul has succumbed to what pride has led him to do, or should I say self-pride.

This emotion in itself doesn't destroy a man's soul; it is what it guides a man to do. When you feel good about yourself, you feel pride. But … if you do something that you aren't happy with, the pride in your heart can make you lie, cover up, deceive, and even murder so the world will not find out what you have done.

When pride is only in the mind, it can be controlled. Other thoughts can keep it at bay. Reasoning and the ability to bring forth the truth can harness the pride from overwhelming the soul. Only when pride enters the heart can it destroy a person's soul. Pride can grow in the heart and take on an emotion that can rule the mind and all other emotions. It can lie to you. It can trick you. It can lead you down a path of deception and eventually destruction. And why, you ask? Because it doesn't want to feel the shameful, burning feeling in the heart when the truth is exposed. To admit wrong is something pride doesn't like. That is why it is so hard for someone to admit sin, or wrongdoing.

Remember, it is the actions of pride that will make you do evil. And when pride enters your heart, you will do anything to prevent the world from finding out your sins. It will make you lie even to yourself, and when you do this, your soul is in jeopardy.

So let's sum it up. Pride is good to have. It makes you feel good about yourself, but it also can lead you to damnation if you let it get into your heart. Once it is there, you allow it to grow until it takes on a new growth. And it will continue to grow as long as you fertilize it with your negative thoughts and actions. You willingly allow it to control you because you fear what somebody might think of you if your sins are exposed.

Sin is an action. Pride is not an action, but it can lead a person to action. And that action can lead you to lie and murder and all those other unpleasant things.

There is one thing you can do to prevent pride from taking over your soul, and that is to repent. That's right: all you have to do is open your mouth and tell the world, or whoever, what sin you have done and ask for forgiveness. It may hurt at first, but in the long run it will prevent pride from devouring your heart and ruining your life.

This is the whole reason Jesus Christ allowed himself to be crucified on the cross: to die for the sins of mankind. By dying this most horrible way and forgiving those who nailed him to that cross, the sins of mankind were forgiven. All you have to do is ask for forgiveness in a public place and the pride in your heart will melt away. Then you can feel a wonderful peace in your heart in the place where pride once existed. It is your choice to believe that or to go on letting pride grow and grow in your heart. It is your decision.

Let's get back to Hitler.

When the pride of life began to grow in Hitler's heart, he was destined to be a man of the Devil. Any man in a high-level position, not just Hitler, is more prone to the temptation to do terrible things than a regular man. To have the power of who lives and dies is a great responsibility. And those who have this power and abuse it will become evil and wicked.

When the people of Germany worshipped Hitler and gave great praise to him, it was easy for pride to enter his heart. No man in history was worshipped by his people more than Adolf Hitler. The spectacular speeches he gave amplified a special love in their hearts and minds. This love they had for their Fuhrer was something unnatural and out of the ordinary. As the pride swelled, it made Hitler a beast, a beast ready for revenge, hate, and murder.

The time now is September 1939. The Devil has developed Hitler into the Antichrist. He has bloated him for six and a half years with the seven deadly sins of emotion. Hitler is consumed with all these sins and now is ready to unleash his evil on the world.

Earlier Austria and Czechoslovakia were taken without a fight. Hitler's sneaky ways and the intimidation of making war was all that was needed to steal these two sovereign nations. His ego must have been enormous after taking them so easily and doing so without firing a single bullet. His plan for world domination has started with the absorption of these two countries.

The Devil has directed him to unleash the power of destruction. Hitler's armies are well armed and well trained. He has made ready to bring war into the world—war like no other in history. Blitzkrieg, or lightning warfare, will be introduced to the people of Poland, and the result will tear that country apart.

Hitler is ready to impose his will on other weak nations of Europe and Russia. And soon the time will be set for the extermination of the Jewish people. This will be Hitler's ultimate goal along with the Devil's, and he will implement it under the cover of war.

Before Hitler invades Poland, he sends a letter to the Soviet dictator, Joseph Stalin, and tells him of his plan to invade Poland. He asks permission to do so.

Poland is the landmass that divides Germany from Russia. If Hitler invades Poland, the Russians will more likely come to its defense. Hitler knows that, so he wants to cover all his bases and get Joseph Stalin's approval beforehand. It is here that Joseph Stalin gives Hitler the scepter to start World War II. Without Stalin's permission, Hitler would never have been allowed to invade Poland.

On September 1, 1939, with the approval of Joseph Stalin, Adolf Hitler invades Poland with an army of 1.5 million troops and does so without a declaration of war. His army easily defeats the people of Poland. Hitler is responsible for the deaths of 60,000 Poles, along with 200,000 wounded and 700,000 captured. It is a cakewalk for the mad dictator. Hitler has his first nation of conquest. World War II has begun.

Ten days after the invasion of Poland, Germany and Russia carve up Poland so each can have their share. The world verbally attacks Russia, but Stalin doesn't give a damn about what the world thinks. He just smiles lightheartedly and allows his armies to take over his part of Poland without a struggle.

Finland condemns the Soviet Union for allowing Germany to invade Poland. They ask the League of Nations to expel them, and they do. Stalin's pride is shaken up so much that he takes revenge. On November 30, Joseph Stalin invades Finland. He eventually overtakes the country but not without sustaining large numbers of casualties. The battle lasts only three and a half months. The Finns put up a determined fight with the help of volunteers from Sweden, Denmark, and Norway. But with the Soviets' massive army, the Finns finally capitulate.

The proud heart and evil mind of Joseph Stalin has been unleashed into the world. He has become a sinister phenomenon to the accomplishment of war. His pride leads him to attack Finland and punish the Finns for having the Soviet Union removed from the League of Nations. His reasoning for engaging in war fits his own agenda. His permission for Hitler to invade Poland makes him the number one master of the warmongers.

After Hitler takes Poland, he moves on and takes Demark and Norway without much resistance. These countries are no match for Hitler and his colossal armies. These conquests are done in early 1940 as the world waits to see who his next victim will be.

On May 10, 1940, Germany goes after Belgium and Holland (the Netherlands).

The blitzkrieg, or lightning warfare, is unleashed on these two countries with complete organization and effectiveness. They are no match for Hitler's war machine. Tanks and planes ravage the territories with terror and complete destruction. By the end of May, both countries surrender.

Soon France surrenders to Hitler. This is the peak of Hitler's accomplishments while he is in power. On June 22 he has the armistice signed in the same railcar in which the German government surrendered in World War I. This humiliation to the French people brings a profound sadness to them like nothing else ever before. The battle of France is over. The hearts and minds of the people of France fall into a melancholy of gloom and despair as the German army occupies their cities.

For the rest of the year, Hitler battles for Britain. He bombs the cities of England without mercy. No strategic objectives are targeted. He bombs and kills innocent civilians by the thousands just for the sheer terror it causes. He tries to bomb the country into oblivion to break the will of the people of Britain so they will surrender. His evil ways simply make the people more determined to fight on and to never surrender. The inner strength of the people of Britain will never yield to Hitler or anyone else. Their strong character and profound faith in their ability to overcome Hitler will forge a new resolution to overcome the yoke of tyranny. They will not surrender at any cost!

By the end of 1940, Hitler still has not invaded Britain. But something more horrendous is happening. He starts to segregate the Jewish people in Warsaw. He rounds them up and puts them into ghettos. This is the first step of the Final Solution. Later they will be exported to the death camps, where gas chambers will be waiting for them.

By the end of April 1941, Greece and Yugoslavia are added to Hitler's conquests. His armies are unstoppable. Hitler's ambition to rule the world gets more real with each conquest. His insane desire to smash the world into submission overtakes all other things now.

The Devil, Lucifer, is happy with Hitler's actions—not just the suffering he is causing but the viciousness growing in his heart. He wants Hitler to hate more and more, and of course, to blame the Jewish people for causing the war. Lucifer wants the lies to grow in Hitler's mind so he will seek retribution. The Devil knows what he is doing. He has molded Hitler into the beast of extermination. He wants his evil subject to render his desires, the desire to rid the world of the Jewish people.

The pride in Hitler's heart is growing and growing. It begins to lie to him every day now. It tells him that the Jewish people are the cause of this war. This lie amplifies the hate until the hate consumes his mind and soul. He is ready to vent this hate by exterminating the Jewish people by the masses. The more he murders, the more the power surges throughout his soul. The gluttony for murder produces a lust for supreme power, all from a twisted lie.

But Hitler has plans that the Devil didn't count on. His monster begins to do things his way, not Lucifer's way. Hitler has plans to invade the Soviet Union and take Stalin's throne. Lucifer doesn't want any conflict with Stalin.

It is Stalin who gave Hitler the scepter in the first place. The Devil doesn't want Germany in a two-front war either. He wants Hitler to move west and take Britain, not the Soviet Union. This act will be Hitler's downfall and eventually lead to his defeat.

Lucifer wants Hitler to lead an invasion of Scotland and Ireland and then arm them to fall on England. Let the Irish and the Scotts lay waste to Britain.

Hitler's war ambition has taken over his intellect and led him to take everything by force. He doesn't realize that he will run out of troops and materials eventually. He needs to recruit others to do the fighting. His madness and compulsion have led him to blindly engage in too many conflicts.

Hitler could have taken Russia without firing a bullet, or maybe without firing many bullets, if only he had turned the people against Stalin. He could have recruited many tens of thousands of men to fight against the communist dictator and sit back and wait for Stalin to die. Propaganda and corruptible ways would have been more useful than all the planes and tanks he unleashed. But no, Hitler had to do it his way, and his way would fail.

On May 10, 1941, the Devil tries one last time to sabotage Hitler's plans to invade the Soviet Union. He deceives Rudolf Hess into flying to Scotland to persuade the English to stop the war and unite to fight against the Soviet Union.

What an idiot he is! How can someone be so stupid to think that Britain would do this? It just goes to show how stupid some people can be when they are deceived.

Anyway, this spoils Hitler's advantage of surprise. The cat is out of the bag. But stupid Stalin can't accept what Hitler was planning. Stalin must have been the most stupid, ignorant, sightless dumb-dumb that has ever lived. He doesn't do anything to prepare for any invasion. He just can't believe Hitler would ever invade his country.

What a moron. On July 30, 1941, Operation Barbarossa is put into action: the invasion of the Soviet Union.

Hitler's armies sweep through Russia like a hot knife through butter. They inflict many casualties while roaring easily through the Russian landscape. In some towns and villages the Germans are cheered and greeted as liberators by the Russian people. But their joy is soon replaced with contempt and hate. The Germans are mean and vicious to all the people. They murder innocent men, women, and children without thought. Their actions are of demons and monsters. They devour everything and everyone in their path. The ruthlessness they show to the people of the Soviet Union is a terrible crime against humanity. The cries of the innocent flood the territory in a wave of consternation and bring horror and sadness like never before.

Hitler gets close to taking Moscow but can't seem to finish off the Russians. The spirit of the Russian people with their strong determination to overcome this conflict is enormous and an inspiration to all others fighting the Nazis.

The madness of Hitler's losses is taken out on the Jewish people. His hate conjures up the substance to bring on the Holocaust at a faster pace. The reality of losing the war does something to Hitler. It amplifies the hate growing in his mind. He blames the Jewish people for all his faults and disappointments. These fits of rage and indignation are disturbing to all who witness them. The Jewish people must pay, he thinks to himself. The dictator of the Third Reich is losing his mind.

On July 22, 1942, the Nazis begin to transport the Jewish people from the ghettos in Warsaw to the death camp of Treblinka. The railcars take these poor souls to their demise. What horrible suffering these people endure on this journey. No food, no water, no place to use the bathroom; they are in complete darkness with the smell of urine and dung overwhelming their senses and adding to their misery. While packed into these hot, sweltering boxcars, they cry out for days for someone to save them. The wretchedness of these surroundings must have been tremendous for these people to endure. The angels in heaven must have wept miserably while this suffering was going on.

The year 1942 is one of death for the Jewish people. Their cries and prayers for someone to save them go unheard. The murder of thousands every day brings on a time of sadness for all of mankind. The gas chambers will be filled to capacity as the toxic vapors from the diesel engines fill the empty spaces. The Jewish people who perish this way are told they are going to have a shower. But the lies make it easier for the Germans to do their evil.

The Devil is finally seeing the operations of his overall plan come to pass. The Holocaust is going on, and the world is shielded from seeing it as the war continues.

The year 1943 is another year of murder for the Jewish people. More death camps are built and used. The Devil has his time. The gassing of Jewish people takes place every day! Their cries continue to be unheard to the world. The trains arrive at the death camps with music playing. The sound eases the minds of the ones fixing to die.

There is a question: if a tree falls in the forest and no one hears it, does it make a sound? When the tree falls, it makes a sound, but if no one is there when it falls, then no one hears the sound. It is only when a person can experience something that he takes notice and hears the sensation of sound. It is only when a person or some other form of life witnesses a noise that it can be acknowledged as being heard.

In every generation there is another type of tree that falls—not a tree composed of wood but one made up of an intangible substance. This substance is contrived with the serenity of the consciousness of society. If that society cares about their fellow man, then they will hear the tree fall. The society that doesn't hear the tree fall is one that doesn't care.

When those innocent Jewish individuals were screaming out for help, the world, as a whole, didn't hear their screams. They didn't want to hear their screams. This society didn't hear the tree fall. Does that mean those screams didn't make a sound?

Here in this time, in this generation, the people of the world didn't really care about the fate of the Jewish people. The tree that fell in this time was not heard. This society did not care about the Jewish community. There were some who did try to help them, but as a whole, the global society didn't care about the fate of the Jewish people. Only when a society hears the suffering of their fellow man do they hear the falling of the tree.

Hearing classical music as the trains arrive at the death camps gives the Jewish people a certain sense of ease. This makes it easier for the Germans to execute their wicked acts. Anything the Germans could do to make murdering easier is implemented.

The men are directed to go one way, the women and small children the other way. They undress thinking they are going to have a shower. Then the doors of the gas chambers are shut and the sound of the diesel engines starts.

How horrible it must feel to be there, scared, naked, in a dark chamber waiting to die, hopelessly hearing the screams and crying of all the others. Smelling the carbon monoxide gas as it slowly enters the chamber. This is a miserable way to die! And so many millions perish this way. How gruesome it must feel.

The death isn't quick. It takes thirty minutes or more for the gas to work. This is done over and over again. The lives of these people are snuffed out in this most horrible way just because they are Jewish. How has mankind been deceived into doing this horrible act? What kind of people could do this? How could this evil be done? The Devil has the answers. Ridding the world of the Jewish people will prevent his demise. He knows the Jewish people will one day bring forth one who will dethrone him. His hate for the Jewish people is something not of this world. He wants the entire Jewish race destroyed. For a time the Devil will get his way, but only for a time.

The year 1944 is no different for the Jewish people. Murder is easy for the Germans now. The deaths of thousands and thousands every day becomes normal.

Hitler grows more hysterical as the war goes against Germany. The world is fighting back with a vengeance. Hitler knows he is losing the war, so he sends more Jews to the death camps as top priority. He sacrifices his military supplies just so the murder of the Jewish people can be carried out more quickly. Now, nothing is more important to Hitler than the destruction of the Jewish race.

The year 1945 arrives with Germany in total retreat. Hitler's armies are failing on every front. Germany itself is in ruins. It is just a matter of time until the Russians overtake Berlin.

Who is this man Adolf Hitler? His life is one of evil, death, hate, and destruction. Was he born to be this horrible man? I believe Hitler was destined by the elements of the past and the reality of the present to become the Antichrist.

One evolves into what he or she becomes in life. The decisions we make as adults guide us down the road of life. Those decisions, right or wrong, make up what we will become.

I think it is easier to do wrong in this world than to do right. It takes discipline to walk down that narrow trail of morality and rectitude and struggle with our demons day to day to live right. We must know how to control our thoughts and behave in a manner that will inspire others to follow our lead, and to show the world who we are by our good works and not just by our words. We have the freedom to choose to walk down the hard road of good or walk down the easy road of evil. The character of our person will be created by the road we choose to take. And God will always be there to inspire us to make the right decisions if we let Him. We only need to find time to listen for His word.

Before World War II began, Hitler was greatly admired throughout the world. He brought Germany's economy to new heights and made it strong, and brought a new beginning to the German people.

Some people believe Hitler was born to be the monster he became. I believe he was born to be the Antichrist and a mass murderer from the very beginning of his life.

There is one thing in Hitler's being that made him a perfect specimen to become the Antichrist. He had the extreme ability to lie to himself. I guess it is this trait that caused the Devil to choose Hitler to become his disciple to rid the world of the Jewish people. He had the perfect ability to be easily deceived.

It some ways we all have an Adolf Hitler in ourselves. We all have the ability to lie to ourselves. When false thoughts run throughout our minds, they may lead us to do things that cause hardships for ourselves and for others.

There are many people in the world now who live their lives as a lie and cannot admit to themselves that they are wrong about things they have committed. When you lie to yourself and hate enters your mind, it begins to control your heart. You are now in the perfect state to do evil. This trait of lying to oneself is something only the individual has any control over undoing.

Before World War I began, there was one who believed the false thoughts in his mind: the leader of Germany, Kaiser Wilhelm II. It was his actions to rescue Lenin in Siberia that led him to have a false sense of security about fighting Russia. He must have thought Lenin could overthrow the czars and then Russia would not be such a threat to Germany. By doing so it was easier to wage war with France. So Kaiser Wilhelm II of Germany was responsible for bringing the Bolsheviks to power. Who knows: if Kaiser Wilhelm II hadn't rescued Lenin from Siberia, he may never have been so bold to go after France. World War I might never have happened!

Germany started World War I. There is no argument to change that fact. Germany invaded neutral Belgium to get at France. By doing so, the Germans escalated the conflict that brought the world in. The German government lied to the people of Germany, saying they had had great victories, when in fact they endured many defeats. When the German armies were near capitulation, they hurried for an armistice.

The lies got bigger when the war ended. The people of Germany just couldn't believe the truth—that they were responsible for the war and that they were defeated. This proud people just couldn't accept that their government was at fault.

It is a terrible thing to lie to oneself, and to think that you are doing the right thing, or God's will, when in reality you are doing the wrong thing. When the wrong thing is mixed up with hate, or any other negative emotion, then violence is not too far away.

Many political leaders and clergy leaders of the world are in that same state now. They have the ability to lie to themselves and use hate to journey down the wrong path, for themselves and for the ones they are supposed to serve. Lying to oneself is probably the worst thing one can do to oneself. It sets the stage for self-destruction and a worthless life.

When evil takes root and starts to grow, the truth is strangled by the vines of lies. Like a disease that destroys the body, a lie kills the ability to see the truth and warps the mind to see things with a twisted overlook. Only believing in God and asking for His help can cure this disease of disdained thoughts. Only with love and understanding and repentance can one open one's mind to see the truth.

To open their minds and see the truth, people must open their hearts and admit their transgressions. To battle the demon of pride, who locks the heart away in the dungeon of darkness and keeps it from experiencing the truth, people must unlock this door with the key of repentance and allow love to flow freely and drown the lies that have imprisoned the soul.

To prove this belief I only have to show what Hitler said in his last days. He feels he was doing God's will and has no remorse for what he did to the Jewish people. He still blames the Jewish people for the war and everything else. His evil mind has nothing but wicked thoughts of hate and misconceptions. His last words will show what happens when a man lives his life as a lie.

Hitler had an insane lust for power, and he used that power for the destruction of an entire race of people. He didn't care about anyone else in this world. This is what happens to a man who lives his life out to be a lie. How many other men, religious leaders, dictators, political leaders, and just plain common men contain this destructive trait in their lives? How many other Adolf Hitlers are out there?

What kind of man was Adolf Hitler? What man could devise a plan to murder millions of people by sending them to the gas chambers? How could he have put that plan into action without leaving his fingerprint on it? There was not one document that showed Hitler ordering the extermination of the Jewish people. He carefully directed people in his organization to do this evil without directly showing any responsibility on his own. There is no doubt that he organized the whole operation. It was his secretive way of doing things that made it so sinister. He knew he was doing evil but didn't want the world to know.

His atrocities were beyond comprehension. His determination to destroy the entire Jewish race was branded on his soul. What kind of monster could create the murdering camps where innocent men, women, and children were gassed to death? Places like the following:

Chelmno. A total of 340,000 died from carbon monoxide gas poisoning.

Belzec. A total of 600,000 died by carbon monoxide gas in the six gas chambers they had. Up to 10,000 people died in one day! It was opened in March 17, 1942. It was the first of the extermination camps that used the gas chambers. This camp was operational for a year and a half until it was shut down in late November 1943. It is hard to comprehend that so many people would be put to death in this fashion and in such a short time, but it really happened.

Sorbibor. Between 250,000 and 350,000 died by carbon monoxide gas in five gas chambers. It operated from May 1942 to October 1943. The rebellion in the camp in October 1943 allowed a couple hundred prisoners to escape. Heinrich Himmler, head of the Secret Police, shut the camp down and ordered that pine trees be planted to cover up what took place there.

Treblinka. This is where 900,000 died from carbon monoxide gas.

Majdanekl. At this camp, 1.3 million people died from carbon monoxide gas in seven gas chambers.

Auschwitz/Birkenau. More than 2 million people died by Zyclone B (cyanide gas) in four gas chambers. Only here was Zyclone B gas used. It was a new type of gas—pellets that became poisonous smoke when exposed to air. All the other death camps used carbon monoxide gas from running diesel engines.

Not only were the death camps real there were also concentration camps where people were worked to death or shot. Altogether there were over 20,000 of these camps created! These places will forever leave a stain on the conscience of all of mankind. The horrible suffering and hardships put on the Jewish people at this time should forever be recorded as the darkest days of mankind.

The inhumanity done to these people should be looked at as a sacrifice so mankind as a whole would not perish from the earth. Later on you will understand more clearly why the Jewish people had to suffer and die in this fashion and why God allowed it.

When a man lies to himself and has the power of life and death, the Devil is in control of that person's soul. These deceptive thoughts are overwhelming and have a controlling nature to that person's actions. But at the end of one's life the truth is the only thing that will save that person.

The following is to show what Hitler's mind was like during his final days. It is important to show how disoriented Hitler was toward the end of the war. The excerpts show exactly what Hitler said in his last will and his last wishes. This is to show how his mind was full of lies and deceptions right up to the very end.

It is April 29, 1945. All have gone down to the bunker of the Reich's Chancery.

The war has devastated Berlin. It is dark and gloomy down here. The air is stale, and the rooms are small and cramped with a darkness of iniquity. There the atmosphere is filled with an eerie force where orgies have been going on. The presence of evil fills the underground bunker.

The war is lost for Adolf Hitler, and his insane quest to rule the world is coming to a close. He is now a broken man waiting for the end to come. He and his remaining partisans are there to be with him to the final end. Hitler orders his secretary, Traudl Junge, to take down his last will and testament. She prepares herself, makes way to Hitler in the dark, grungy quarters, and takes down the Fuhrer's last words.

Hitler's Political Will

More than 30 years have passed since I made my modest contribution as a volunteer in the First World War which was forced upon the Reich. In these three decades, the love of, and loyalty to my people alone have guided me in all my thoughts, actions and life. They gave me the power to make the most difficult decisions which have ever confronted mortal man. I have spent all my time, my powers and my health in these three decades.

It is untrue that I or anybody else in Germany wanted war in 1939. It was wanted and provoked exclusively by those international statesmen who were either of Jewish origin or worked for the Jewish interests. I have made too many offers of limitation and control of armaments, which posterity will not from all time be able to disregard, for the responsibility for the outbreak of this war to be placed on me. Further, I have never wished that after the appalling world war, there should be a second one against either England or America. Centuries will go by, but from the ruins of our towns and monuments, hatred of those ultimately responsible will always grow anew. They are the people whom we have to thank for all this: international Jewry and its helpers.

This is a complete lie. Even during Hitler's last days, he couldn't bring the truth to the surface. He says he didn't want war in 1939, nor did any German for that matter, but he had German criminals shot and dressed in Polish uniforms and placed around a German radio station. He then arranged a phony takeover of the station by supposedly Polish soldiers. He wanted it to look like Poland was the aggressor and was invading Germany. He did this so he could righteously invade Poland and look like he was avenging the aggressor nation. At the time he thought it was funny, but later, when the war grew more intense, he blamed it all on the Jewish people. It was here that his hatred for these people grew. This testament Hitler made shows how he was so caught up in his lies that he couldn't see that he was responsible for starting the war.

> Three days before the outbreak of the German-Polish war, I suggested to the British Ambassador of Berlin a solution of the German-Poland question, similar to that in the case of the Saar under international control. This offer, too, cannot be denied. It was only rejected because the ruling political clique in England wanted the war, partly for commercial reasons, partly because they were influenced by propaganda put out by international Jewry.

How ridiculous this is! He thought England wanted the war for commercial reasons? This is the dumbest thing I have ever heard. Hitler really believed the international Jewish community was behind wanting of this war. His mind was polluted with lies.

> I also made it quite plain that if the peoples of Europe were again to be regarded merely as pawns in the game played be the international conspiracy of money and finance, then the Jews, the race which is the real guilty party in this murderous struggle, would be saddled with the responsibility for it. I also left no one in doubt that at this time not only would millions of children of the European Aryan races starve, not only would millions of grown men meet their death and not only would hundreds of thousands of

women and children be burnt and bombed to death in the towns, but this time the real culprits would have to pay for their guilt, even though by more human means than war.

After six years of war which in spite of all set-backs will one day go down to history as the most glorious and heroic manifestation of the struggle for existence of a nation, I cannot forsake the city which is the capital of the State. As our forces are too small to withstand the enemy attack on this place any longer, and our own resistance will be gradually worn down by men who are blind automata, I wish to share my fate with that which millions of others have also taken upon themselves by staying in this town. Further, I shall not fall into the hands of an enemy who requires a new spectacle, presented by the Jews, to divert their hysterical masses.

I have therefore decided to remain in Berlin and there to choose death voluntarily at that moment when I believe that the position of the Fuhrer and Chancellor itself can no longer be maintained. I die with a joyful heart in my knowledge of the immeasurable deeds and achievements of our soldiers at the front, and our women at home, the achievements of our peasants and workers and of the contribution, unique in history, of our youth which bears my name.

That I express to them all the thanks which come from the bottom of my heart is as clear as my wish that they should therefore not give up the struggle under any circumstances, but carry it on wherever they may be against the enemies of the Fatherland, true to the principles of the great Clausewitz. From the sacrifice of our soldiers and from my own comradeship with them to death itself, the seed has been sown which will grow one day in the history of Germany to the glorious rebirth of the National Socialist movement and thereby to the establishment of a truly united nation.

Germany wasn't united by the National Socialist Party. It was this political party that divided Germany. Those who didn't accept what the government said were sent to a concentration camp where they were worked to death or shot. To unite a people you don't take away their freedoms. Hitler and his party of radicals did just that. The freedoms of the German people were taken from them, and in turn they became slaves to Hitler and his twisted ideological way of thinking.

Many brave men and women have decided to link their lives with mine to the last. I have asked and finally ordered them not to do this, but to continue to take part in the nation's struggle. I ask the commanders of the armies, or the navy and the air force to strengthen with all possible means the spirit of resistance of our soldiers in the National Socialist belief, with special emphasis on the fact that I myself, as the founder and the creator of this movement, prefer death to cowardly resignation or even to capitulation.

May it be in the future a point of honor with German officers, as it already is in our navy, that the surrender of a district or town is out of the question, and that above everything else, the commanders must set a shining example of faithful devotion to duty until death.

These are the words of Hitler. Fight until death even when there is no hope of winning; sacrifice your life for a worthless cause. This shows what kind of man Adolf Hitler was, wanting his fellow countrymen to continue to fight even though there was no chance of winning.

A war of conquest, a war to kill and destroy, a war to smash the world into submission, but most of all, a war to segregate the Jewish people in controlled areas so they could be shot or gassed—Hitler's goal was to exterminate the entire Jewish race under the cover of war. This is what he called a faithful devotion to duty until death.

The annihilation of two-thirds of the Jewish people by genocide in Europe was carried out by this man and his henchmen. No man in history has ever stained this world with the blood of so many innocent people like Adolf Hitler. This is why I think Hitler was the Antichrist. How can anyone deny this claim? The only ones who can are those who choose to lie to themselves and deny what Hitler did. They in turn become their own Adolf Hitler.

Hitler married his mistress, Eva Braun, on April 29, 1945. This is what Hitler said about her in his last will:

```
Although during the years of struggle I
believed that I could not undertake the
responsibility of marriage, now, before the
end of my life, I have decided to take as
my wife the woman who after many years of
true friendship, came to this town, already
almost besieged, of her own free will, in
order to share my fate. She will go to her
death with me at her own wish, as my wife.
This will compensate us for what we both
lost through my work in the service of my
people.
```

I wonder if Eva Braun ever knew about the Holocaust. It's a pity that such a young, beautiful girl like Eva Braun would die with the most hated and most sinister man Germany had ever seen. She was captivated by Hitler's charismatic influence. I wonder how she feels about him in the afterlife, now that she knows what Hitler did to Germany and the world while he was in the service of his people.

On April 30, 1945, the man named Adolf Hitler ends his wretched life by biting down on a cyanide capsule and pulling the trigger to his gun, sending a bullet to his evil brain. The Antichrist is dead.

He lived to be fifty-six years old. He reigned as supreme leader of Germany for twelve years and three months. His life was filled with evil and damnation to the entire human race. He is responsible for the deaths of 48 million people, along with the murder of 6 million Jewish individuals. More than 3 million German soldiers gave their life for their Fuhrer. Billions of dollars' worth of property was destroyed. Europe itself lay in ruins.

Why did this have to happen? Why was this man allowed to do such evil? Where was God when Adolf Hitler was making his destructive plans for the world?

Sometimes even God is prevented from stopping such things, because if He did something to intervene, then maybe something worse would come to pass. God was helpless to stop Hitler. God was helpless because of another man waiting to inflict more destruction than Hitler. Where was God when Adolf Hitler was making his destructive plans for the world? He was preparing heaven for the arrival of those Jewish souls.

Who was this man Adolf Hitler? The world has been changed by this man for the worse like no other before him. So much killing, so much murder, so much hardship, so much misery was created by this one man. What kind of man was Adolf Hitler? No man can deny it. It is plain to see. Adolf Hitler was the Antichrist.

CHAPTER 5

The Creation of the King of Evil

SIMILAR TO THE ANTICHRIST was another who was created to do more evil to the world. He possessed political ambitions and ruled with brute force. It was because of this man that God was put into a stranglehold, unable to prevent the Antichrist (Adolf Hitler) from carrying out his evil plan, the so-called Final Solution.

This man was equipped not only with a mighty army but with a political theory to try to enslave the world. He was dangerous for what he could do physically, but he was even more dangerous for what he could do without firing a shot. His political power cornered the world and seduced millions of people to fall for the biggest scam ever brought to the world. This scam tried to enslave the world and jeopardize its freedom. The seductive nature of this political theory robbed many nations of their freedoms. It gave men visions of paradise like a narcotic but delivered only suffering and hardship and murder. It is this political theory that gives this man the title King of Evil.

The Devil has been trying to rule the world ever since mankind has been on Earth. He has tried with violence and war making to divide and conquer so misery and suffering would be the norm, to trick mankind into doing his bidding with enticements of temporally worldly pleasures—anything so he can control the world. He realized that to conquer the world and keep it, he had to come up with a way of life that would be alluring and seductive to its inhabitants, at least at first, until he had complete control and there was no outlet to change the system.

The Devil came up with this political theory and had the perfect man for the job. This theory was communism, and the man to ring in this new order was Joseph Stalin.

But before communism could be brought about, it originated in a more watered-down theory. That theory came from Karl Marx and became known as Marxism.

Karl Marx started the road to communism. Its first stage was simple: luring the world into believing that this theory would take care of every basic human need. The government would control all things and provide for the general public.

The government would have total power over everything. It would proclaim that it would take care of the people. Also, it would guarantee that everyone would live free from poverty and disarray. The government would provide you with a job and a place to live, and literally take care of everyone's needs. All would live under one set of rules: no rich, no poor—all would be the same. This way numbs whole societies from becoming free to do what each individual wants and pacifies entire countries to keep them from growth and social development. Such a society is stagnant, with no hope of anything new and fresh except what the government can provide. This was only a theory at the time Karl Marx drew it out. It took someone else to refine it and put it into practice, and that person was Vladimir Ilyich Lenin.

Lenin refined it and call it Bolshevism. He tried to make it a new way of life in Russia, but first he had to overthrow the czars. Revolution came to Russia near the end of World War I in October 1917. Lenin instated this theory to the people of Russia. He installed this new theory for seven years. He numbed the intellect of the people with his philosophy of Bolshevism, much like using morphine. He was the man who took Marxism out of the textbooks, refined it, and then put it into practice.

But Bolshevism needed to be refined one more time. After Lenin died in 1924, another man took this theory to the next level. He made it his own: his way was to completely take away the freedoms of the people of Russia and have complete and total control over them and the government, to rule the biggest country in the world uncontested, and to turn Bolshevism into the most concentrated form of this political party: communism. The man who inherited the reins of power and made it his own was Joseph Stalin.

This political theory grew into being like the poppy plant. The poppy plant produces opium. When refined, it produces morphine, and when it is refined more, it produces heroin.

Karl Marx was the cultivator of the political plant that became a scourge to mankind. Marxism acted like opium. It numbed the intellectual spirit and made the individual become a slave to it; once a slave, a person would give up his or her freedoms easily without the will to fight for them. When you experience opium, it does the same thing, and as time goes by, you become a slave to the substance.

Vladimir Lenin refined the opium like political party into Bolshevism and brought it to life. When he took over Russia and installed this political theory as the one government of the biggest country in the world, Russia, he concentrated this opium way of life and made it stronger, like morphine. The addiction happened quickly, and soon all the people of Russia were hooked on this political way of life. But still it would be concentrated one more time.

When Lenin died in 1924, Joseph Stalin took over the helm of power. He concentrated this morphine like political government to make it his own. He refined it so he and only he could have total power over the government. He strengthened and concentrated Bolshevism into the heroin like political structure called communism. Now that it was refined to its max, one man could rule completely without question and without anyone to stop him.

When Joseph Stalin took over the government, he was forty-five years old. His lust for power had come. He brought with it a theory of control that would suppress millions of people. Communism was the realm in which to have complete and total power. This power took on a new meaning of control—not just the control of the people or the country, but with it the substance to create the ambitions of conquering the world. Not just some of it, or most of it, but all of it, and to do so with the controlling nature of heroin.

This was the Devil's last political attempt to conquer the world, to conquer and maintain control of every square acre of land. From the North Pole to the South Pole, from the east to the west, no country would be immune to the influence of the heroin like political theory of communism.

If and when this political party would be established and instated as law, all religions would be removed from the earth. There would be no churches left. They would all be torn down just like Stalin did when he took power in 1924. Worshipping God would be against the law. Religion as we know it would soon fall into the abyss. Men of faith would be imprisoned and then killed, just like they were when Stalin was in power.

This is why Joseph Stalin was so dangerous. He was not just a man with a large army with the ambitions to rule Russia; he reserved in his mind an intangible substance that was so powerful, he could enslave and then rule the world. Communism was that substance.

When Stalin came to power in 1924, he ruled with an iron fist. It is estimated that he killed 20 million of his fellow countrymen by the time of his death in March 1953. No man had the power Stalin had.

More of the atrocities Joseph Stalin did to the people of Russia before World War II will be told later. They were some of the most horrible things imaginable. It is hard to believe one man could bring so much horror and misery to his own people.

Russia was a nation made up of hardworking, simple people. They were a people with strong determination and a modest character. They didn't deserve to be treated so harshly and cruelly. The people of Russia, when Stalin was in power, were the most innocent victims of the Devil's purge to rule the world. Only when Hitler created the Holocaust was there more innocent bloodshed and misery put upon a people.

Stalin was born Joseph (Iosif) Dzhugashvili on December 21, 1879. On the old-style calendar, this would have been December 9, 1879. He changed his name to Joseph Stalin in 1910. His mother called him "Soso." She wanted him to become a priest, but instead he became one of the meanest, most vicious men of all time. He became a monster to his people. He stole and murdered and raped his country with ease. His image was like that of a god, but behind doors his wickedness prevailed in secret. He gave Adolf Hitler the authority to invade Poland and by doing so started World War II.

He ruled a country of 147 million people when he came into power in 1924, with 3.5 million more born every year after.

His word was law, and no one challenged his authority. He attained something no man had ever achieved: complete and total power over the country he ruled. Looked upon by his people as someone to worship or venerate, he in turn used this adornment to forge a new understanding of evil in the world. How could this be? How could a people blindly give in to one man to completely rule? One must go back to see how this came to be.

Before the Revolution of 1917, the people of Russia had become distraught about their government. The czars had segregated themselves from the people. The privileged ones in the government lived the life of millionaires, whereas the rest of the people barely had enough food to eat. The people had had enough of being neglected. They wanted a new way of life. That new way was about to blossom with a man named Vladimir Lenin.

His words were seductive. The people ate up what he was preaching. His way would provide everything for all the people. His new government would provide food for all and a place to live and everything else. His words brought about the Revolution.

People wanted change. They wanted the government to care about them and do for them. In the present state, the czars had completely alienated themselves from the people. The people were talked into overthrowing the government and ridding them of the czars once and for all.

Lenin put outrage into the people and in turn brought about violence. He distorted the truth and used the people's misery to amplify the force he needed to take over the government. He did so at a time when the masses' anger was at an all-time high and they were hungry—a perfect time to plant the seeds of evil. No one had any respect for the present government, and change was something the people were ready to accept. It was the perfect time for revolution.

In Lenin's mind he thought he was doing the right thing. He really believed that the government could provide for all the needs of the people and take care of them.

The main element that intoxicated the people so easily is that they wanted someone or something to provide for them. Bolshevism promised that. The people didn't realize that they had to give up their freedom to acquire this new way of living. And once they gave it up, there was no turning back. They would have to do what the government told them to do. This is why Bolshevism—later called communism—was conceived by the Devil and implemented to the masses by men eager for power.

When Lenin got sick in 1924, he looked to find someone to take over. He was very reluctant to turn things over to Stalin. He didn't think Stalin was cut out for the job. He even warned others to be wary of Stalin and said he shouldn't be trusted. I wouldn't be surprised if Stalin had something to do with Lenin's death. No one will ever know, but as ambitious as Stalin was and given that Lenin didn't really like him, it would be understandable for Joseph Stalin to murder Lenin to achieve power. Anyway, after Lenin died, Stalin took over and became the leader of Russia.

It is hard to believe one man could do so much evil and murder so many innocent people, but he did. The reader might find it hard to believe the following about who Stalin was. It might sound too far-fetched and too horrible that one man could do these things. But I reassure you that the following account of what Stalin did to his fellow countrymen and to the world is completely true. What he did was real. This is to show the character of who Joseph Stalin really was—a man with complete authority in a totalitarian political state that allowed him to be the King of Evil. His strength was like heroin that was derived from a single political poppy seed. His overwhelming power gave him complete control over his people. The people of the largest landmass of the world became his chattel and were subjected to the harshest form of forced labor.

Three years after Stalin seized power, he started to industrialize Russia on a scale not ever seen by any nation. These industrial projects were done by enslaving his people and forcing them to do back-breaking labor.

One of those projects was to build the White Sea/Baltic Sea canal. A total of 150,000 men died building this canal! The work was inhumane. The men would be worked to death. This was just the beginning for the Soviet people of what would come from Stalin's complete control and vicious decrees.

During the 1930s Stalin took all the land and made it his, in a process called "collective labor."

He enslaved 10 million people of Russia in the disguise of Soviet communism reform. Those who refused or rebelled against this new way of life were thrown in prisons. This brought on the infamous time of the Gulag.

The people of the Ukraine were the ones hardest hit by Stalin's new laws. He took everything from them. While 5 million people starved, he exported millions of tons of grain. He needed money to pay for his industrial projects, so he stole all he could. How could any man inflict this kind of law on simple peasants? He did it because he could, and anyone who didn't go along with his plans was murdered.

The situation in the major cities was different, especially in Moscow. As long as the people submitted to Stalin's decrees and did what they were told, everything was fine.

He would not tolerate anyone who threatened his power. There were those who got too popular with the people; Stalin would have them murdered. He took no chances. Anyone who was a threat to Stalin was killed, even if it was someone he liked.

His uncanny knack for self-preservation was one of Stalin's strongest talents. He was also a master of manipulation, maintaining his public image while all these murders were going on.

I guess when a man has the authority to have people killed for any reason, there comes a time when the value of life doesn't mean anything to him. Then he kills more and more until his conscience is destroyed. Having the power to murder thousands a day without any thought of who those people were gives new meaning to evil. That person with power becomes a different form of human being. He thinks he can do anything, and without anyone stopping him, he continues with the sense of being a god.

Stalin's sense of self-preservation was so strong that even people whom he liked couldn't withstand his wrath. On December 1, 1934, Stalin had a man named Kirov murdered. Stalin loved Kirov, but he was getting too popular with the people. Kirov bragged about and supported Stalin with complete obedience. His complete and total devotion to Stalin was like no other. His faithfulness was true and complete. Why then, why would Stalin have this young, ardent man and most devoted colleague killed? The only reason is his insane jealousy and his profound attempt at self-preservation. He was a threat to Stalin's power, so Stalin had him killed—not just Kirov but anyone and everyone who wanted to replace Stalin with Kirov. This would bring on the bloody purges. *Purge* means "to clean up," and that is what Stalin would do, clean up the Politburo, using murder on a scale never before known.

Stalin didn't know which party members supported Kirov, so he shot everyone who was close to him. More than 1,100 party members were rounded up and sent to the Gulags, where most were shot. This time was recorded as the Great Terror.

Within two years 1,500,000 people were murdered by Stalin. As many as 1,500 to 2,000 innocent people would be killed each day in Moscow alone. This was the character Joseph Stalin was.

People in the Gulag would write Stalin and tell him of the horrible suffering they were going through. They never knew that it was Stalin who had arranged to put them away. He was a master of manipulation. He put the image to the Soviet people that he was a saint and a great provider. The people worshipped Joseph Stalin like a religious figure. In the homes of the people were portraitures of Stalin looking grand and baronial, but it was he who caused all the suffering and death to these guileless people. This is the character of Joseph Stalin.

His relationships with women were no better. On November 8, 1932, celebrating the fifteenth anniversary of the Bolshevik Revolution, Stalin and his second wife, Nadya (Nadezhda Alliluyeva), had a fight. The next morning she was found shot to death. She was only thirty years old, and the mystery surrounding her death will never be known. But Stalin was probably the killer. He would get away with another murder. He was immune from prosecution.

His relationship with his mother was also bad. He didn't care much for her. She tried to raise him up in a religious fashion. She sent him to a Catholic school when he was fifteen years old, in hopes that he would become a priest. He hated the school and was thrown out years later. His mother did everything in the world for him to turn out right, but all her actions turned him against her. Stalin's mother died in 1937. He did not attend her funeral. He visited her only one or two times in the last forty years of her life.

I am writing this about Joseph Stalin so people will know how evil this man was. The character of this man was like that of a monster to his people and the world. His atrocities are unmatched by any other evil men who ruled without a conscience. It is very important to tell the world how evil this man was, and to describe what he did so the world will know why—why the Holocaust had to happen as it did. By knowing who Joseph Stalin was, the world will have a better understanding of why God had to let the Jewish people perish in the Holocaust.

In 1939, Adolf Hitler sent Stalin a letter. He was going to invade Poland and wanted his permission to do so. Hitler promised Stalin he would carve Poland up and said Stalin would benefit tremendously if he allowed him to do this. It was then that Joseph Stalin gave Hitler his authority and his permission to start World War II. It was Joseph Stalin's agreement not to come to the aid of Poland that allowed Hitler's armies to overtake the country without any interference. Stalin gave his consent gladly. It was Stalin who gave Hitler his scepter to bring war to the world.

Then, after Hitler invaded and conquered Poland, Stalin did some invading himself. Stalin took Estonia, Latvia, and Lithuania without much resistance. When you are mightier and much better equipped than your opponent, it is easy to impose your will on them. And that is just what Stalin did to these small countries. His desire to conquer and rule had been established. He was ready to continue his conquests and satisfy his appetite for overtaking the weak and the small.

After Hitler's conquest of Poland, Stalin directed his army to take Finland. He didn't like the way Finland reacted to Hitler invading Poland and how the Soviet Union hadn't done anything to stop him. Stalin didn't like being accused of conspiring against the people of Poland. So at the end of November 1939, Joseph Stalin invaded Finland.

It was a battle of 2 million Russians with 5,000 airplanes against a meek 200,000 Finns with only 150 airplanes. It was not a fair fight to say the least. The Finns did put up a courageous fight, but in the end, Stalin forced them to surrender. The big bully of evil got his way, and another country was converted to a communist satellite.

Stalin, happy with himself and bloated with power after taking four small countries, made ready to devise his strategy to conquer more lands and more people and more souls.

When World War II started, he was the master of 192.5 million people. He was the absolute master of the largest landmass on earth. The raw materials he controlled gave him everything necessary to build his armies without foreign help. He was in the right place to take small nations, one at a time, at his leisure. The world was within his grasp, and he was ready to clench his fist and pound the world into submission. All the others he would seduce with the intoxicant of his political theory. He was truly the King of Evil of the world.

The Devil had finally found a way to merge religion and politics to forge a new order. Not with a religious leader in charge of political matters and the government, but with a new political party (Communism) with the seduction of a religious fervor.

Stalin became the religious figure people needed to worship. He became God-like to his people. He was all the religion the people needed, so he abolished the church. He burned the churches to the ground. He was the only one to be worshipped now. In his own mind he became God.

Hitler was destined to be the Antichrist because of the outcome of World War I. His false hatred toward the world became an obsession with revenge. He blamed others who were not at fault to elevate his hatred and then used the Jewish people as the ones who should be punished for the humiliation of losing World War I. Germany brought into power this corporal to save them, and by doing so set the stage for the Holocaust.

Stalin on the other hand was created to be the monster he turned out to be. Communism had to evolve before it could be imposed on the world. If it hadn't been Joseph Stalin, it would have been someone else. The doctrine of communism would dictate and guide whoever was in charge of the Soviet Union at this time. The Devil had all this planned many years ago. The two dictators would create an environment that not even God could stop. If God had done something to intervene, something worse would have happened. That will be defined later. The Devil planned his strategy carefully. He was waiting for God to intervene so he could use Stalin to destroy the world. If he couldn't rule it, he wanted it destroyed. The Devil is real. God is real. The showdown of these two dictators was about to change the course of history, and the Jewish people were right in the middle of the carnage.

CHAPTER 6

The Primary Islamic/Jewish Conflict

One would think that this would be the longest chapter in the book, given all the anger and hatred these two groups have for each other. I have researched and studied long and hard the reasons why these two religious groups don't like each other. Here are my findings.

With the conflicts, hate, violence, and other abominations between these two faiths, I can sum it up in one thing: Jerusalem. The Islamic world hates the Jewish people because they control Jerusalem. It is believed that the prophet Muhammad ascended to heaven from here. It is for this reason that the Islamic world wants to control and have Jerusalem as theirs and not share it with anyone else.

It seems fatuous that all the hate and violence in this part of the world stems from one religious group wanting to have total dominance over this city.

Why can't all three major religions share this part of the world and live in harmony? If one of three totally controls this city, then the other two will fight for all time until they overtake it. They must all share Jerusalem with the Jewish people as overseers of their capital.

Jerusalem is the divine section that makes Israel complete. There can be no Israel if there is no Jerusalem. This city must remain in the hands of the Israelis.

The Islamic world, the Jewish world, and the Christian world must find common ground and stop fighting over Jerusalem.

CHAPTER 7

The Jewish Faith, the Islamic Faith, and the Christian Faith

THE JEWISH FAITH

I should call this part of the book "The Jewish Race and Faith" because the Jewish people are a race of people who developed a religion. Practicing the Jewish faith doesn't necessarily make you Jewish. Who is a Jew? Is it someone who practices the Jewish faith? The answer is no. You must be born into this world from Jewish parents. It is the race, not the religion, that makes someone Jewish. Most people believe it takes only the mother to produce a Jewish child. That may be acceptable since she brought the baby into the world.

Let's go back to Abraham to see how the Jewish race came into being.

First of all, Abraham, or Abram, was not Jewish. He was not Arab. He was a man who was obedient to God. And it was God who chose Abram and Sarah to bring into the world the Jewish and Arab races. Sarah and Abram created Isaac and in doing so created the Jewish race. It took two people to bring about the Jewish race. Abram and Hagar created Ishmael and in doing so created the Arab race.

This is like the question of which came first: the chicken or the egg. Neither. Look at it this way. It takes a chicken to lay a chicken egg. But say an animal—not a chicken—mated with another animal—also not a chicken—and then produced an egg. Say that egg hatched but the animal did not become like either the mother or the father; instead, it became a different form of life. Then that animal grew up and mated with its siblings. After a few generations a chicken would evolve.

Abram was the first part of this subject. It took Abram and Sarah to produce Isaac. This union produced a new race—the Jewish race. Abram first mated with Hagar out of wedlock and produced Ishmael, another different race.

My point is that Abram wasn't a Jewish man. Sarah was not a Jewish woman. But when they mated, they brought about a child. This child grew up and started the Jewish race. That is how it all started.

As long as a baby born into this world is born of a Jewish woman, that child is Jewish. It seems simple to me. Even if the woman is only part Jewish, any of her offspring will become Jewish. I am glad that matter is cleared up.

Then there is this myth of having to be circumcised to be Jewish. No. No. No. Circumcision is just a ritual that Jewish people do. It is a tradition they practice that is part of their religion, not their race. Just being circumcised has no way of making someone Jewish. I am glad I cleared that up for you individuals who are confused about this subject.

There are other scriptures that say that if someone is obedient to God, that makes them Jewish. Wrong. It is fine if one wants to be obedient to God, but that doesn't make them Jewish.

If one is descended from Isaac, then he is part Jewish. If one's parents are both Jewish, then any children from this relationship will also be Jewish. There are many who have Jewish blood in them but aren't really Jewish. It can get quite complicated. It shouldn't matter if someone's great-great-grandfather was Jewish.

Throughout the centuries Jewish blood has been mixed with other races and creeds. So what? It really isn't that big a deal. It is just something that has taken place.

The bottom line is that God chose Abram and Sarah to bring a new race of people into this world. Abram was chosen because he was obedient to God.

I believe the angel Michael had something to do with Abram's DNA makeup. I think it was Michael, along with the other angels, who helped

God create the many races of mankind. Abram was just one of those individuals made to form the Jewish race. I think Michael made the traits necessary for the Jewish people to come into being. I think the angel Michael created this race of people so that one day they will bring into being one who will capture Lucifer and put him into bondage for a thousand years—the Jewish messiah. And he won't be Jewish. I think Michael is somewhat responsible for the creation of Abram and doing so the Jewish race.

Let me make this perfectly clear: like I said earlier, Abram was not Jewish. I hope I am not offending anyone, but if so, too bad. It is time you know the truth. Abram and Sarah created Isaac, who was the first Jewish person.

Sarah was just as important to the creation of Isaac as Abram was. Women were all too often neglected in the Bible. It is here that Sarah should get her recognition.

God joined Abram and Sarah in holy matrimony. They were married in God's eyes. This makes their relationship sacred! Isaac was the first true Jewish man ever created, period. Remember, it takes two human beings to bring a baby into the world. It took two people to create a baby who became a new race, and this race was the Jewish race.

When Abram fathered Ishmael, he wasn't married to Hagar. This relationship was not sacred. It was not in God's eyes, so He wouldn't recognize any offspring. That is why Ishmael is not Jewish. He is his own separate race—the Arab race.

It really doesn't matter if someone recognizes someone else as being Jewish. I am sure many of us have Jewish blood somewhere in our bloodline. You can really get technical about this matter if you want. Just look at it like this. Look in the mirror and be honest with yourself. If you have Jewish ancestry in your family, if you have Jewish features in your makeup, if you think you are Jewish, then you are. What you feel as a person is all that matters. If you think you are Jewish, then convert to Judaism and forget what others think and be Jewish. Be yourself. Be the person you think you should be and leave the world to accept that.

And being Jewish doesn't mean you can't be a Christian too. Anyone can be a Christian if they believe that Jesus Christ suffered and died on the cross for the sins of mankind. Remember, the first Christians were Jewish.

Don't stop there. You can be a Muslim also. You should be able to belong to any and every religion you want to. God is not a dictator. Religion is just a way to worship or be close to God. Anyone can belong to all the religions of the world if they choose to. Remember, religion is like a club, and you can belong to more than one club if you so desire.

People might look at you and judge you unjustifiably for not belonging to just one religion. When this happens, just look them in the eye and say, "God isn't a Muslim. God isn't a descendant of Abraham. God is not Jesus." (Many will disagree with you about that last point. Jesus was a man who sacrificed his life for the sins of the world. He was a man who became a savior, but he was not God.) "Religion was made up by man. I can belong to any religion I want to, because I love God and I don't want to be left out from any group that worships or loves Him. I am a free man [or woman]. I am free to choose my salvation. I am free to dwell with all others who want to be close to God. I am free to choose my many beliefs and discard what I don't want to believe. I am not a robot who must believe what I am told. I believe I have the right to belong to one or all religions, because I am a man with the desire to love God not by intimidation or force, but by my own free will, because I am a free man. I believe God wants all men to worship and love Him freely. And that's why I belong to other religions, because I have the freedom to do so."

Now that we have that matter cleared up, let's get to the faith of the Jewish people. Anyone can belong to the Jewish faith. It doesn't make you Jewish, but you can worship God through this religion if you wish to.

JUDAISM:
THE RELIGION OF THE JEWISH PEOPLE

To practice Judaism is to practice the Jewish faith; to read and accept the Jewish Bible, or Torah, is the foundation of this belief. The Torah strengthens your faith with God by the prophet Moses.

Religion is like belonging to a faith club. Everyone in that club must follow certain rules and regulation. They have traditions and customs they practice. This way of living brings together the members of this club. Anyone can belong to Judaism if one wants to accept its rules and regulations. If people don't practice these rules within the guidelines of this religion, they can be thrown out, just as they can be thrown out of any other club or organization.

I am not going to tell about all the traditions and practices of the Jewish faith. I am not trying to get anyone to convert to Judaism. I am just explaining what this faith represents.

The hardships of the Jewish people and all they went through to become a proud people deserving of God's love and the love of the world should be recorded. Their religion is a reflection of who they are and what they did for the world. They should be recognized as a people with strong determination who suffered greatly so the world would not succumb to the damnation of the Devil.

Understanding the scriptures of Moses primarily makes up Judaism. The five books of Moses alone with the Old Testament give Judaism their faith and spiritual guidance in God.

The Ten Commandments that Moses brought down from Mount Sinai are very important. Here they are:

1. You shall have no other god besides me.
2. You shall not worship any idols.
3. You shall not misuse the name of the Lord your God.
4. Remember the Sabbath day by keeping it holy.
5. Honor your father and mother.
6. You shall not murder.
7. You shall not commit adultery.
8. You shall not steal.
9. You shall not give false testimony against your neighbor.
10. You shall not covet anything that belongs to your neighbor.

These are the basic things God wants us all to abide by no matter what faith we belong to. It is here that God has set forth laws so mankind can live right in His eyes. Judaism is the religion that came from the Jewish race. No matter what religion we belong to, we are all God's creations. We should all believe that there is one God, and that God loves us all and wants the best for us.

The Islamic Faith

I hope this chapter will open up the eyes of people who are confused about the Islamic faith. Many believe this faith is full of violence and hatred, but in reality that is false. Islam is quite the opposite. It is against violence and many other despicable things that are going on in the world. It was the 1979 revolution in Iran that started the misconceptions and distortions about this faith.

What is a Muslim? It is someone who belongs to the Islamic faith. What do the Muslims believe in? They believe that there is one creator and only one ruler to judge over the universe. In other words, they believe there is only one God. This is called monotheism. They believe in prophets. One of them is the prophet Muhammad. There are other prophets they believe in too. They also think Jesus was a prophet.

There are many interpretations of Islam, but there are primarily two groups of Muslims: the Sunni and the Shia. The percentages are 85 percent Sunni and 15 percent Shia. There are nearly six times as many Sunnis as Shiites. There are about 1.2 billion Muslims in the world. They make up the world's second largest religion after Christianity.

The Sunnis have dominated the Shiites in most countries. The Sunnis believe leaders should be inherited, whereas the Shiites don't feel this way at all; they think their leaders should be judged or accepted for their intelligence, not by who their ancestors are or what they did. This is primarily why there are two different groups within Islam.

People don't always agree when religious or political ideology is discussed. You see, the individuals within ourselves emerge from what group or groups we belong to. Not all Muslims think the same. Not all Jewish people think the same. Not all Christians think the same. No matter what groups, or what religion, or what political organizations we belong to, the individual in us makes us special.

All people are different. We look different. We think differently. We act differently. We are different. When we get involved with religious or political organizations, we are trying to belong to something that will bring us together as human beings and make us whole. These groups bring us together but not totally, because we still are all different. Just because we want to worship God the same way doesn't mean we have to go along with everything we are told. We as people cannot dissolve our own unique individuality.

Some people think that when you become a Muslim or a Christian or whatever, you must go along with everything you are told. You must give up the right to think for yourself. You must go along with the crowd and do as you are told. You are enticed to give up your individuality. We must never do this! Religion can turn people into robots. Religion can warp our minds about what is wrong and make it appear right. As long as a person can think for himself or herself, he or she can avoid being a victim of deception.

The individuality in us keeps us from becoming molded together and controlled. We should always be able to think for ourselves. Our intelligence should override religious doctrines that someone may impose on you. We should keep God in the proper perspective and not let others sway us the wrong way because of their religious beliefs. If you don't acknowledge something is right, don't be intimidated and go along with the crowd.

Now let's get back to the Muslim faith and Islam.

Like the Arabs, Muslims think they came from Ishmael. This is not just a religion but can be looked on as a race of people also. But only 20 percent of the Muslims in the world are from Arab countries.

In the sixth century the prophet Muhammad received his revelations from God through the angel Gabriel. He felt he had the testament to correct human error. This testament is the Qur'an. Muhammad was not the founder of Islam, only one of the three prophets.

Moses was the first prophet Muslims believe in. Through him and the Hebrew scriptures, the Torah, they got their beginning. The second prophet was Jesus, through the four Gospels, and then finally there was Muhammad, through the Qur'an. These three prophets make up the Islamic religion. I bet most of you didn't know that.

Muhammad isn't the one who created Islam; he was just a reformer for the religion. He thought Christians and the Jewish people were being led astray and that Islam would lead them back to the right track. *Islam* means "path of God."

The word *Qur'an* (or the Koran—they are the same book) means "recitation." Muhammad was not the author of the Qur'an. As a matter of fact, he was illiterate. It took twenty-three years for the 114 chapters of the Qur'an to be written. The entire scripture was finally collected about twenty years after Muhammad died.

Another note: Muslims don't worship Muhammad; they worship God. Muhammad is just the prophet who showed or brought the path of God to them. This is important to know. God is the focal point in this religion, not any one man.

It is said that Muhammad was married many times. I don't think anyone knows exactly how many, but the one wife who stands out is the one he spent most of his life with. Her name was Khadija. They were married for twenty-four years until her death when Muhammad was forty-nine years old. They had six children: two boys who died in infancy, and four girls.

There are five core beliefs that all Muslims believe in. These things are called the Five Pillars of Islam. They are as follows:

The first Pillar of Islam is the Declaration of Faith. There are two parts. The first part means one is to accept that there is only one God. The second is that Muhammad is the messenger, or prophet, of God.

That is what a prophet is, a messenger from God. This declaration is known as *Shahada* (witness, testimony).

The Islamic name for God is Allah. The Hebrew name for God is Yahweh. The Christian name for God is God.

The second Pillar of Islam is Prayer (*salat*). A Muslim must pray five times throughout the day: at daybreak, at noon, at midafternoon, at sunset, and then in the evening.

They pray not just to God but to remind themselves that there is only one God, Allah. Doing this five times a day reminds them to believe in only one God. This is very important to Muslims. It may sound redundant to others, but to constantly remind themselves that there is only one God and one God only is something that keeps them believing. This is the second Pillar of Islam.

The third Pillar of Islam is called the *Zakat*, which means "purification." It requires Muslims to give 2.5 percent of their wealth. That means total asset wealth, not just annual income. With Islam a person doesn't own things. It is God who owns those things. So Zakat is really the act of charity. It is not limited to the 2.5 percent. The Shiite group pays more to the religious leaders. It is like a religious tax to help with the poor.

The fourth Pillar is the Fast of Ramadan. This occurs once a year in the month of Ramadan. It takes place in the ninth month of the Islamic calendar. Muslims must not eat, drink, or engage in sex from dawn to sunset for the whole month, health permitting.

The fifth Pillar is the Pilgrimage to Mecca in Saudi Arabia. At least once in their lifetime believers must make the journey to Mecca. The pilgrimage season follows Ramadan. More than 2 million people make this journey to Mecca every year.

Once there they shout, "I am here, O Lord, I am here." They are then instructed to go to the Kaaba. It is inside the compound of the Grand Mosque. The crowds of people there move counterclockwise around the Kaaba seven times.

There are many rituals the people do, but I am not going to go through all of them. I am not trying to convert anyone to any religion. I am just giving the reader a better understanding of the three main religions.

The Kaaba is the most sacred place in the Muslim world.

Mecca, in the country of Saudi Arabia, is the birthplace of the prophet Muhammad.

Muslims believe in heaven and hell and angels, and that there is a spiritual and physical afterlife.

Like I said earlier, Jesus is looked upon as a prophet, but Mary, the mother of Jesus, is also prominent in Islam. As a matter of fact, Mary is the only woman called by name in the Qur'an. Mary is mentioned more times in the Qur'an than in the New Testament. Muslims regard Mary highly and revere her as one who completely submitted herself to God's will. Muslims believe in the virgin birth.

It is better to tell you what the Muslims don't believe. They don't believe Jesus is the Son of God. They look at him only as a prophet, not a savior. They do not believe in the crucifixion and the resurrection.

Muslims don't believe there is a need for someone to die for their sins. They think that everyone will have to answer for their own sins to God. God will judge each person for what they did and how they lived. It will be His decision whether to forgive your sins. In other words, you will be held responsible for your own salvation. They don't think Jesus, Muhammad, or any other man can be responsible for your sins.

Sunday is the day most Christians go to church. Muslims go to congregational worship on Friday at noon.

Who are the "fundamentalists"? It seems like they are the violent people in Islam. There are extremists in every religion, in every political party, or for that matter, in any group where the people think with a single point of view. Fundamentalists or political Islam got its start in the late 1960s. This is what happens when you mix religion and politics. You get one group that thinks with one perception on all matters. And when a group of people starts to force this one way of thinking on others, then anger, hate, and violence can occur.

Not all fundamentalists are violent. Many political Islamic activists are nonviolent throughout their entire lives. They include professionals with college degrees who try to improve political and social problems. But when they get caught up with the ways of the world, it can lead to extremism.

That is the bad part of religion and politics. When the two are separate, they can be reasoned with. But when you combine the two in one mind, it can consume the intellect, and then distortion can overtake the truth, resulting in violence.

I see and hear on TV and read in the newspapers about suicide bombers blowing up innocent people, thinking they are doing God's will. This is totally wrong. God would never want anyone to end their life just to kill someone they don't even know. The people who encourage this madness will suffer greatly one day. They must answer to God for deceiving these lost souls into engaging in these evil acts. Using any religion to do evil and perform acts of violence will be exposed one day, and the shame will burn like fire.

All people with hate in their hearts and minds will have to answer for their actions. There is no excuse for bringing violence into this world just because people can't handle their hate. Hate is something that grows in the mind until it consumes the heart and then devours the soul.

It is trickery that a man does when he thinks up false things. These false things conjure up hateful ideas. Then these ideas, which might sound good at first, turn on him and begin to deceive or lie. Then the individual begins to believe these lies as truths. They are distorted by voices or thoughts of false things. This cycle continues until hate becomes like a forest fire burning out of control. Those hateful thoughts are believed to be right, when in fact, they are false. So when the individual commits horrible acts, like blowing up someone or killing someone, that person feels like they have done an honorable act. These people are only fooling themselves. In their distorted minds they can't see the truth. Inflicting pain and suffering on their fellow man just so they can go to heaven is selfish! To expect that they will receive forty virgins and live in paradise as an outcome of evil violence is simply egocentric.

It is hard to stop thinking hateful things once hate has become a normal way of life. I think that if you could add up all the bad things the average man has thought about in his lifetime, the total would be more than all the sand particles on all the beaches of the world. Only truth and love can stop hate from growing.

I pity those extremists who kill themselves thinking they are doing God's will. They are not martyrs, just murderers led astray. They will not go to heaven. They will not experience paradise. They will not spend eternity with God. They will not see heaven—not because God won't allow them in but because they will be too ashamed to enter heaven's pearly gates once they are shown what horrible people they were when they lived in this world.

No religion will save you from your actions. You must admit to them before you can get any forgiveness. Those who perform ghastly acts of evil will be punished, not rewarded. Where there is sin and violence, there is deception. And it is this deception that turns men into monsters. It is deception that the Devil has used to reign over this world. But you can be sure that those who commit acts of violence and kill innocent people will be looked at as the Devil's apostles and not as God's holy warriors.

There is a difference between fighting for one's beliefs and murdering innocent people. Just because one is mad at the world, that doesn't give one the right to harm others.

Men have fought to remain free since the beginning of time. To fight someone who is a threat to your loved ones or to protect your country is justified. Killing those who try to take away what we hold dear is cogent and right. It is not a sin or wrong to kill someone if there is a threat to survival, or to save others. Those who lay down their lives to save others are martyrs. Those who kill in acts of terrorism are not martyrs. They are simply deceived individuals who have a twisted way of thinking. They think they are doing right, but they are deceived by the intoxicant of religion.

The people who trick and deceive those into committing these acts will one day suffer God's worse castigations. Those individuals will be looked upon as the worst of the worse. They will be damned and never feel any peace and joy and love from God. For all of eternity they will be lost souls too ashamed to admit their sins.

Wherever there are two religions, or one religion that has been divided, there can be extremists ready to inflict violence and bloodshed. As long as they think they are right, they will think they are serving God. A man will hear only what he wants to hear and discard the rest. Only the truth can clear the smoke of distortion. One should never let religion become an instrument to drive a wedge between God and man. Religion is supposed to be a way to worship or love God, not a means by which to inflict suffering on the innocent.

Islam is a peaceful religion. It came to pass to make people's lives content. It was designed to bring people closer to God and make this world a kinder and gentler place. When extremists try to impose their one way of life, one government, and one way of believing in God on others, they start to poison the whole concept of Islam.

The conflict going on in Iraq is appalling, with Muslims fighting and killing other Muslims. The quarreling amongst the Sunni and Shiite factions is against everything Islam is about. Innocent people being killed by each other without any reasoning is simply evil. What kind of people can blow up themselves and others just so they will go to heaven? This is wrong. To die for a cause is one thing, but to die because you are unhappy in this world and want to go to heaven is against what God wants. You have only one life to live in this world; to end it by self-destruction will only make God unhappy.

The Muslims have many traditions and customs. I don't need to go over all of them. I am not trying to convert anyone to any religion. I just want to explain to others who know nothing about Islam how peaceful Islam is. It is only when extremists enter the picture that violence is created.

THE CHRISTIAN FAITH

There was a man who gave his life for the sins of the world. He suffered and died miserably nailed to a cross; for nine long hours he suffered this way. He was a carpenter by profession until he started his ministry at age thirty. He lived to be thirty-three years old, and his name was Jesus.

Christianity is a simple religion. It doesn't forbid you to eat or drink anything. It doesn't require you to dress a certain way or perform certain rituals. All Christianity requires is for followers to believe in Jesus Christ as the savior of all mankind, to believe in his teachings, and to believe that he died on the cross for the sins of man. It doesn't require anything else.

One must come to Jesus, not the other way around. It is a free religion. Nobody is going to pressure you to worship Jesus. Nobody is going to come to your house and make you go to a church or any house of worship to pray. There is no pressure to become or stay a Christian. Worshipping, believing, and practicing Christianity is simply up to the individual who chooses to do so.

There is so much to write about Jesus: his birth, his teachings, his parables, his apostles, his trial, and of course, his crucifixion and resurrection. I could fill volumes just on this one man's life. I will try to explain the most important things in a brief, concise review.

He was born in 3 or 4 BCE to Mary and Joseph in a humble setting—in a stable near an inn. There was no room at the inn, so Mary had her son born in the stable. Mary laid Jesus in a manger (Luke 2:7) in the city of David.

We celebrate his birthday on December 25, but this is not the true date of Jesus' birth. Some think he was born on August 2, but this date could also be wrong. It isn't the date he was born that is important but the fact that he was born. He was born into the world of the Virgin Mary.

Right after his birth, Mary and Joseph went to Egypt so the evil King Herod wouldn't kill Jesus. After Herod died, they came back and lived in Nazareth.

Jesus started his ministry when he was thirty years old. He was baptized by his cousin John the Baptist. John knew that Jesus was the

Christ the world had been waiting for. He baptized Jesus to consecrate the beginning of his ministry.

After Jesus was baptized, a voice from heaven was heard saying, "This is my son whom I love; with him I am well pleased" (Matthew 3:16–17). This is where Jesus is looked on as the Son of God.

Jesus performed many miracles. He gave the blind sight. He gave those who were lame the ability to walk. He cured those who had leprosy. He made the deaf hear. He performed many miracles, and because he did, there were those who used these wonderful things to persecute him.

One of the greatest things Jesus did was teach us how to pray. Prayer was very important to Jesus. After he performed a miracle, he would go somewhere and pray. He told us not to pray like the hypocrites standing in the synagogues and the streets where they would be noticed. He wanted us to pray when we were by ourselves. "But when you pray, go into your room, close the door and pray to your Father, who is unseen" (Matthew 6:6). He taught us not to pray just for ourselves but also for others. He wanted us to pray for those who do us wrong, to pray for our enemies. This is something only Jesus could have asked us to do.

I guess the most important things about Jesus, besides his suffering and dying on the cross, were his teachings. He taught us to love one another, that the life we live in this world is only temporary, and that eternal life is more important and to prepare for it. To tell of all his teachings would take way too many pages. Here are some of them:

Anger Matthew 5:21–26
Divorce and remarriage Matthew 5:31–32; Mark 19:1–12; Luke 6:18
Eternal Life Matthew 19:16–30; Luke 10:25–37; and John 3:1–21; 18:18–30; 4:1–41; 5:19–47; 10:7–30; 12:44–50
Faith Matthew 18:6–9; Mark 11:20–25; and Luke 17:5–6; 21:18–22
Forgiveness and sin Matthew 18:21–35; Mark 1:14–15; Luke 7:36–50, 26:26–29; 17:1–4, John 8:1–11
God John 3:1–21; 8:12–30
Happiness Matthew 5:3–12; and Luke 6:20–26; 11:27–28

Judgment Matthew 11:20–24; and John 12:44–50; 12:32–42; 25:31–46

Kingdom of God Matthew chapters 5–7 and chapters 20–25 Matthew 18:1–5; 19:13–30; Mark 1:14–15; Luke 13:18–30; 18:18–30; John 3:1–2; 19:11–27
Love Matthew 5:38–48; Luke 6:27–36; and John 13:20–35; 10:25–37; and chapters 14–17
Obedience Matthew 7:24–2; Luke 8:11–18; and John 14:15 and chapter 17
Peace John 14:27–31
Persecution Matthew 10:16–25; John 15:18–27
Prayer Matthew 6:5–15; Mark 11:20–25; and Luke 11:1–13; 21:18–22; 18:1–18
Resurrection Matthew 22:23–33; Mark 12:18–27; Luke 20:27–39
Worry Matthew 10:26–31; Luke 12:4–7; John 14:1–14
Worship John 4:1–26

The teaching Jesus is most remembered for is the Sermon on the Mount. It is here where Jesus tells us of the Golden Rule: "to treat others as you would like to be treated." The Beatitudes constitute one of the most compelling scripture passages. Here it is.

THE BEATITUDES
"Blessed are the poor in spirit, for theirs is the kingdom of heaven. Blessed are those who mourn, for they will be comforted. Blessed are the meek, for they will inherit the earth. Blessed are those who hunger and thirst for righteousness, for they will be filled. Blessed are the merciful, for they will be shown mercy. Blessed are the pure in heart, for they will see God. Blessed are the peacemakers, for they will be called sons of God. Blessed are those who are persecuted because of righteousness, for theirs is the kingdom of heaven. Blessed are you when people insult you, persecute you and falsely say all kinds of evil against you because of me. Rejoice and be glad, because great is your reward in heaven, for in the same way they persecuted who were before you" (Matthew 5:3–12).

It is in this sermon that Jesus tells us to love our enemies. Also, here is the Lord's Prayer and many other things that tell us to show compassion to our fellow man.

It is this man who was crucified on a hard, rugged, painstaking cross. He did suffer long and hard. He did die in this horrible way (death by suffocation), gasping for breath as his body pulled down his ability to breathe. He suffered for nine hours like this! He died this way so mankind wouldn't suffer eternal damnation.

Jesus had twelve disciples. These men followed Jesus and learned from his teachings. They believed in him until one betrayed him—Judas Iscariot. These are the others:

Simeon, called Peter: He was the brother of Andrew, who initially introduced Jesus to Peter. Peter was a fisherman. He had spiritual insight; he knew from the first time he met Jesus that he was the Christ. He was the one who denied Jesus three times the night the Romans came after him. Earlier he told Jesus, "Even if I have to die with you, I will never disown you" (Mark 14:31). He witnessed the crucifixion and later became a fearless preacher for Jesus.

Andrew: He was the first disciple to follow Jesus. He is the one who introduced Jesus to his brother Peter. He told him, "We have found the Messiah" (John 1:41). He was also a fisherman.

James (the brother of John): Peter, James, and John were the three disciples within Jesus' inner circle. He too was a fisherman.

John (the brother of James): He was the only discile to stand at the foot of the cross where Jesus was crucified. He is the one who take care of Mary after Jesus died. He is the disciple Jesus said he loved. He helped in the family fish trade.

Philip: He was called to follow Jesus, not as part of a pair, but as an individual. During the Last Supper, Philip said to Jesus, "Lord, show us the Father and that will be enough for us" (John 14:8). Jesus responded that they had already seen the Father in him.

Bartholomew: He was called Nathaniel by John (John 1:45). Not much is written about Bartholomew. He was one of the quiet disciples.

Thomas: Thomas will always be remembered as "Doubting Thomas," because when the other disciples told him that they saw Jesus alive after the crucifixion, he doubted their word.

Matthew: He was a tax collector. He left his job for good when Jesus called on him to follow him. He is the author of the first book of the Gospels in the New Testament. Being a tax collector was looked upon as something terrible. Tax collectors were in the same category as prostitutes. Not many men even associated with tax collectors. It was not uncommon for the other disciples to despise Matthew, at least at first.

James (son of Alphaeus): There is not much mentioned about this James. He may have been Matthew's brother, because they both were sons of a man called Alphaeus.

Judas (surname Thaddaeus): This is not Judas Iscariot. It is a different Judas. He is not the Judas who was Jesus' brother. He is also not the Judas of Galilee. There are not many references to him in the Bible or any other text.

Simon: He was known as a "Zealot," which means "fanatic or enthusiast." He probably was a member of the Jewish resistance movement against the Romans. Not much is mentioned about him. More likely he was a militant until he became a follower of Jesus.

Judas Iscariot: This is the man who betrayed Jesus. Why would someone do this? Judas Iscariot probably became jealous of the other disciples, and when he didn't get the attention he wanted from Jesus, he turned against him. He may have wanted to see if Jesus would perform some mystic or necromantic powers over the Romans while imprisoned. He was in charge of the money for the disciples, like a treasurer, so maybe he wanted to find a way to get some money. He betrayed Jesus by leading the Romans to where he was for thirty pieces of silver. After he did this, he realized he had made a grave mistake and took his own life by hanging himself.

These were the men Jesus called on to follow him. These twelve disciples who loved Jesus became his strength. They gave him the courage by fellowship to carry out his mission for the world. They were the first Christians and the first to fully understand who Jesus was and is.

After Jesus was crucified, they were called on to be the apostles, a word that comes from the Greek verb meaning "to send." They were instructed to be sent out to the world and preach the gospel of Jesus Christ. They became Jesus' appointed representatives.

What does it mean to be a Christian and live the Christian life? First, believe that Jesus Christ died on the cross for the sins of man. Believe in him and his teachings and that he is the Son of God. Jesus is the way to God. It is through Jesus that you will know God and have a relationship with God.

Another thing is to find time to listen to what God wants you to do with your life. Set aside time every day to let God put ideas in your mind and allow your spirit to receive His message. Then do what God wants you to do. When God wants you to do something, it probably will be something you don't want to do. It will be something difficult to accept. You will have to make sacrifices and deny yourself things. It will be something you will not want to do, but you must be courageous and do it anyway. I guess that is why people don't want to receive God's message; if they do, they will be asked to bear a hardship. But in the long run, if you are obedient to God, you will have a more meaningful life.

When you pray, pray to receive His message rather than just asking for things. Ask for forgiveness through Jesus for what you have said and done; ask Him to lead you from temptation, pray for your enemies—at least some of them—and thank Him for all He has done for you. This is how to know God.

This is Christianity. Acknowledge the teachings and spiritually feel the pain and suffering Jesus Christ went through. Then you can enjoy peace and solitude, knowing that somebody loved us enough to suffer and die for our salvation. Believing in Jesus Christ and his teachings is what Christianity is all about.

SUMMARY OF THE THREE RELIGIONS
(Islam-Christianity-Judaism)

MY PERSONAL FEELINGS ABOUT ISLAM

I think religion is very important in most people's lives. We believe in God primarily so that when we die, we can go to heaven. I think this is the main reason we believe. God is something we believe in because of faith. My definition of *faith* is believing in something that you have no proof is real, believing without knowing all the answers. Nobody can prove there is a God. We believe in God because of our faith that there is a heaven waiting for us when we die.

As long as people believe in something, that something is real. As long as people believe in God, God is real. You can't prove there is a God and you can't prove there is a heaven, but as long as we believe there is, there is.

The terrible thing is that most people believe in God only for the hereafter. God is most useful while we are still alive. He can show us what He wants from us and how to make our lives meaningful. God is much more than just someone to pray to.

I see the Muslim community benefiting from their religion only in terms of what lies after death. I wish the leaders of Islam would not use their religion to get back at others when personal reasons arise and hope they will not.

I see Bin Laden as someone who turned the world against the United States, hiding behind the shield of Islam and deceiving those who have bad feelings toward America. He got his feelings hurt when he was rebuffed by his own country, Saudi Arabia. In the 1990's Saudi Arabia allowed the US Military to come into their country to protect their vital interest. Bin Laden wanted the government of Saudi Arabia to let his army be the saviors of his country. He was rejected and turned on the United States like a rabid dog. He then deceived his followers to hate the United States for reasons other than the one he had. His trickery and deceit are the reason those eighteen young men who aggressively attacked the World Trade Center and the Pentagon on September 11,

2001, committed acts of murder. Those men thought they were doing God's will, but in reality they were doing evil by Bin Laden's deceiving ways. It is people like Bin Laden who used a peaceful religion to turn its followers into terrorists.

In 1979 when the Ayatollah Khomeini took over Iran, he too used Islam to conjure up hate, and by doing so he turned people away from God. He used Islam to put hate into the hearts and minds of the people of Iran for his personal reasons.

He was imprisoned by the shah of Iran and then put into exile.

When the shah, who was nothing but a vicious dictator dressed up in elite uniform, was deposed, the people looked for someone else to take his place. When they found the Ayatollah, they thought they were finding someone to lead them to a better life, someone who could establish an Islamic way of life that would bring the people of Iran together. What they got was a man full of indignation, vengeance, and hate.

He hated the shah and the ones who supported him while he was in power, the United States. For this reason the Ayatollah hated the United States. He then used the Islamic religion to coalesce the people into one group. He used hate and aversion to bring together this group so he could poison it. He chanted hate like no one else. He turned Iran into a nation of hatemonger's. This is what happens when one individual has the influence to contaminate the minds with hate. Nowhere in the Koran does it say that it is okay to teach people to hate.

This is the main problem with Islam: a totalitarian state is made up of one religion and no political parties, one way of thinking, one way to worship God, one way to live. This is just not right! God is not a dictator and should not be governed by a man from any one religion. This goes for any religion, not just Islam. No religious group should control the political spectrum and livelihood of an entire population.

It is believed that 170,000 Iranians were murdered after the Ayatollah came to power. Anyone who didn't go along with the new doctrine was killed. There was no freedom of speech. There was no freedom of religion. There was no freedom of anything. You did what you were told and had better not complain. You had to go along with what everyone did. The people were molded into this one way of thinking.

The Ayatollah did nothing but give Islam a black eye. I think Muhammad would totally dislike what the leaders in Iran have done with Islam. Islam shouldn't teach hate. Islam shouldn't promote the destruction of Israel. Those who use Islam to segregate, and then bring so much unnecessary violence into the world, are not doing God's will.

The extremists who try to force their way of thinking will never establish goodwill in the world. The hate that grows in their minds and lives in their hearts will only bring destruction to themselves and to their eternal souls.

MY PERSONAL FEELINGS ABOUT CHRISTIANITY

Here are my personal feelings—yes, my personal feelings—about Christianity. It is here that I get a chance to express my feelings about what I feel more strongly about than any other thing in my life. Here is my testament on Christianity.

My belief in God is through Jesus Christ. I think he is the man who died for my sins. His teachings are profound. He is more like God than any man who has ever walked the planet. I think he is the Son of God, but is not God.

He was a man of flesh and blood. He felt pain and joy like any other man. He was human and took it on himself to pay the price for the sins of all mankind. He is my savior. Here is why I love Jesus Christ so much.

I think that when we are born into this world, we each have a soul. This part of our being will never die. It will live forever somewhere, either with God or without God. I think everyone will go to heaven when they die. What kind of God would throw us in a pit of fire for all of eternity? I think that is a lot of hogwash. I believe if you don't get to heaven, it is because you choose not to go.

Now, why would someone not want to go to heaven, you ask. I think that when we all stand before the Almighty on Judgment Day and view our lives, many a man will run away because they are too ashamed to witness what they said and did in life. There will be many, and I mean many, who are too ashamed to admit the wrong things they did even when they are shown these actions.

Instead of admitting those shameful acts of fornication, paying for abortions, lying and stealing, and doing those horrible things to those they love and those who love them, and all those many other things that were shameful and wrong, they will run away and live in another place—a place where God isn't present and where they don't have to answer for those acts they have willingly committed: hell.

Eventually they will end up living with the Devil. The Devil, Lucifer, isn't in hell yet, but one day he will end up there with all the others. And when the Devil gets there, he will not rule or reign there; he will be just another worthless piece of shit taking up space.

But the Devil will be waiting for those who turned against God. He will continue to deceive and try to make a place for himself and his angels. But first he will be captured and then bound for a thousand years, the Bible tells us. To live in a place for all of eternity without God would be hell.

That is where Jesus comes into the picture. He knew there would be many a man and many a woman who would never admit to their wrongdoings. They would rather end up in hell first. Jesus knew he had to sacrifice his life so others could repent and not perish. It was his decision to be the sacrificial lamb to suffer and die for the sins of mankind.

I said earlier that Jesus was the Son of God, not God. I need to explain this. I believe there is only one God. When John the Baptist baptized Jesus, a voice was heard: "Here is my son, with whom I am well pleased." You can't be in two places at once. God is in heaven and Jesus is in the water. I don't want to take anything away from Jesus, but I must emphasize that no man is God. No man can ever be God. No man can achieve God-like qualities. I don't care what is written in the Bible. I don't care if I have offended anyone. The fact remains the same, which is that Jesus was a man, not God, period.

Sure, Jesus was crucified, but what makes this act dying for the sins of man? When Jesus was crucified, he was first flogged, and then he was made to carry that very heavy cross. Then he was nailed to it, then he was spit on and laughed at, then they pushed a crown of thorns on his head causing excruciating pain, then he hung there for nine hours, then he asked for something to drink and they gave him vinegar, and then right before he died, he looked up to heaven and said, "Forgive them, Lord, for they know not what they do." This is where Jesus took on the sins of the world. It is here that Jesus forgave the Roman soldiers for their despicable acts toward him. He forgave them. He didn't curse them or curse God; he forgave them instead. This is what the crucifixion is all about. It isn't the words or teachings that saved mankind; it was this act of love and forgiveness that made Jesus the Christ.

Now, the resurrection. I believe Jesus was resurrected from the dead on the third day. I believe he came back in the spirit, not in the flesh. I feel this has been misconstrued all these centuries. Jesus shows us by his resurrection that there is an afterlife. He wanted us to know that after we die, any and all of us, we will have a new life. It is important to understand that the resurrection isn't some magic act being performed, or some sideshow at a carnival. A dead man rising on the third day after he was crucified sounds mystic and like sorcery to some. You might miss the meaning of the resurrection. When he arose, in the spirit, on the third day Jesus showed that there is a new life after we die. He wants us to know that so we can prepare for this new life. He wants us to let his blood wash away our sins so we won't be denied our right to live in heaven after we die. That is my belief.

We all live in this world as human beings. We laugh and love and enjoy all the things life has to offer. But there will come a day when we must leave this world and then answer for all those bad things we said and did. We must admit that we did them and then have them forgiven. Then we can live this new life—this life of eternity. Christianity is the way to prepare for that new life. Jesus is the way to God. And I love him for sacrificing his life for my sins.

My Personal Feelings About the Jewish People

I feel I have written this book for you. I know the sacrifices you made to keep this world intact. I hope you all find peace and good fortune all the days of your lives. You are my inspiration. I feel that Jesus did something for me and now I can do something for you. This book is my testament to all the suffering you have experienced. For you people who have been treated badly and been persecuted so horribly, I just want you to know that God hasn't forgotten you. He knows your character, as a whole people, and thinks that you will not hate Him for allowing the Holocaust to happen. Maybe after reading this book, you will all understand why. Keep the faith and don't ever turn against God. You are the hope of the world.

CHAPTER 8

Why Does God Allow Bad Things to Happen?

A CHURCH BUS CARRYING a group of youths to a concert at a retirement home is involved in a traffic accident, resulting in many deaths. A father of five small children is randomly shot while pumping gas into his truck. An elementary teacher with twenty-four years of service is raped in her home and then stabbed to death. I could go on. There are so many more horrible things that happen to good people. The world is a violent place. There is a lot of meanness in the world. When these bad things transpire, people with confused expressions on their faces look up to the heavens and say out loud, "Why, God? Why did you let this happen?"

Some would say God has a reason for these things. We as humans cannot understand why bad things happen. We try to understand. We search for answers so we can accept these tragic events. Does God have any reason for allowing some children to be killed in a car wreck? Of course not: when these things happen, they happen because deception has entered the picture.

There is one power over which God has no control in this world. This power is deception. When these terrible things I just spoke about happen, it is because man has been deceived into doing them. Bad things happen because of the distorted thoughts growing in one's mind.

Deception is the number one reason bad things happen to innocent people on this planet.

Also, God cannot be every place every time something bad happens. God doesn't have hands. God doesn't have feet. God doesn't have a mouth. God doesn't have a direct way of communicating to anyone in the world. So God can't reach out and save someone when they are in turmoil. But we have hands. We have feet. We have a mouth with which to communicate. We can do God's work. We can be His hands that reach out and touch the world. We can run to the needs that people have. We can tell the world what God would want us to say. We can be the arms and legs and the voice of God. We are God's creations, and we are the ones who can do the will of God. The problem is that not everyone wants to do these things.

The most important thing is not to blame God for these bad things. God is always right. We must all accept that. If something bad happens to us, we must not blame God for allowing it to happen. Until all the answers are given to us, we shouldn't hold any grudges against God. This "blaming God" way of thinking is self-destructive. This is how the Devil turns man against God and later wins over his souls.

We must trust God in *all* things. This isn't easy, and it isn't going to be easy. When the heart is heavy with sadness and grief, it is hard to look at things with intelligence and understanding. One must accept the bad things that happen in the world. We must believe that God is in complete control of the situation. We must not question His judgment or hold any grudges against Him. God is right in all things. That is why He is God.

When bad things happen to us as individuals, such as when a parent dies or a close loved one passes on, we feel the pain with intense emotion. When something bad happens in the larger world, we feel less hopeless. Yet we ask ourselves, what is going on in the world? Why are people fighting with so much discontent? Why are so many people suffering in the world? We feel hopeless as we search our souls for the answers.

Why does God allow famous people to be assassinated? Why are there so many wars going on? Things happen in this world because man is in charge. Men or women decide to do things that have violent consequences tacked on to their decision making. Remember something: it isn't God doing these things, it is man or acts of nature.

Why do hurricanes slam into populated land areas? Man decides to build houses in areas where hurricanes have been before. I hate it when I hear that a hurricane has destroyed an area and people call it an act of God. This is an act of nature, not an act of God! He didn't make and direct those storms to destroy anything.

Hurricanes are created by heat, and heat must move. When it does, it forms storms, and when the storms get more heat from the oceans, they become hurricanes. This is an act of nature, not an act of God! Nature is something that must be accepted for what it is. To blame God when God had nothing to do with it is simply ignorant.

When you see hungry, starving people in the world, it isn't God's fault. It isn't God making them suffer; it is man making them suffer. In every country there are governments that are supposed to look out for the people who empowered them. But when men control the government through dictatorship and corruption, the people are neglected. When the government is not a government of the people, for the people, and by the people, there will be suffering in the population.

God doesn't cause wars to happen; once again, man creates wars. When you see fighting going on, there are two factions in disagreement. One wants to take over the other. When people are not treated right, rebellious groups emerge. Governments do not like rebellions. Government officials want to rule and control everything. The innocent people are caught in the middle. As long as governments do not look out for the needs of the people, violence will soon follow. There will be those who try to change the system. But as long as dictators and evil minds in power the good will be unfairly killed off. Simple human rights should be respected in all governments of the world. Until all governments of the world unite under the system of democracy the world will have problems of injustice and mayhem.

One of the Devil's main plans is to keep misery going on in the world. Making people miserable and unhappy keeps violence and mayhem active. Turning man against man and causing havoc is necessary for evil to grow. Satan isn't going to let peace happen if he can prevent it. He wants to inflict pain and death so he can recruit more souls to his side and so the ones killing the innocent will be his one day.

There is no place more appealing to Satan than the Middle East.

The Middle East is a very complicated area. For a region to live in peace and harmony, most of the people have to get along. In the Middle East there is too much division around religion and not enough respect and understanding. There needs to be a common ground on which all people, no matter where they live or how they believe, can agree to tolerate each other. There are too many angry minds willing to unleash hostilities without first trying to resolve their differences through peaceful means.

For a country to survive and overcome hardships, it must have an honest, respectable, upright government with a strong moral foundation. For a faithful government to function properly, it must be impartial. It can't take sides when dealing with people. To be effective and serve all the people, it must separate church and state. How people believe in God should not take precedence over running the affairs of the state. When government officials take sides over someone's religion, they create resentment. You can't treat all people the same when one religion is favored. A government cannot be effective unless it treats all the people of the country the same and without bias.

As long as the governments in the Middle East are controlled not by political parties but by religious groups, then anyone not belonging to that religion will be ignored and treated unfairly. Religion has no place in politics! Politics should be governed by political parties, and those parties should be made up of people with different religious beliefs. A Republican can be Catholic or Jewish or a member of Islam. A Democrat can be Catholic or Jewish or a member of Islam. That goes for any political party.

The individuals who make up and belong to the political parties should decide how politics should be run. When a single religious group holds the power in political matters that government can be warped and jaundiced to do things with prejudice and malice to those who don't think on the same level as they do. Religion can stagnate a government and end up taking away basic human rights without knowing it. This is not what God wants. God is not a dictator! When men control people through religious institutions, they make God theirs. And no government should control God and use Him to control the minds and hearts of the people. People should be free to choose who they want to lead their government. As long as religion dominates the governments of the Middle East, nothing will change their unfortunate situation.

There should be a separation of church and state, but God should be welcome in all parts of life. God is God. Religion is not God. Religion is a way to believe in God. To separate God is to separate the truth. As long as men and women who govern religious and political matters can acknowledge that there is one God and that their belief will not prejudice their decision making toward others, there will be beneficial and meaningful leadership in that institution.

As man rules the world, God's ability to do anything to stop him is limited. God works through those who are obedient to Him. Those who put God first do what He would want. To serve God and do His work one must be willing to offer oneself totally. One must be willing to be God's voice so the world can hear His word, to be God's hands so one can reach out and touch those who are suffering, and to be God's legs so one can run to the needs of the world. Serving God is not easy. One must deny one's self and sacrifice. This is what the Jewish people did during the Holocaust. They were chosen to suffer and die so something worse wouldn't happen to the world.

God allows bad things to happen so worse things won't. There are bad things that happen that God allows. For example, there must be a reason God did not prevent John F. Kennedy from being shot in Dallas on November 22, 1963, a terrible incident.

John F. Kennedy was probably the most important man to have ever held the office of president of the United States of America. I say this because of what he prevented from happening. This great man prevented a nuclear exchange from the Soviet Union in a time when nuclear weapons were in place in Cuba, an event known as the Cuban Missile Crisis.

In 1962, the Soviet Union was building sites in Cuba to hold nuclear missiles. When President Kennedy was told of this, he had to find a way to get those sites closed down. He was told by his military advisers to simply bomb them. This would have provoked the Cubans into retaliating along with the Soviets. This was a very difficult time to be president. He had to do something. He couldn't allow nuclear weapons to be ninety miles from US shores.

He didn't bomb the sites. He stood up to the Russians and put a naval blockade around Cuba. Anything going in had to be searched by the Coast Guard. Anything and everything military that would have been used to build these nuclear sites was turned back. No ships from Russia would be permitted to enter. Kennedy held his ground, and the Russians finally understood that these sites had to be disassembled and taken down.

John F. Kennedy got those missile sites taken down without using violence. Many years later it was revealed by retired Soviet military leaders that if they were attacked at sea that they would have retaliated with short range nuclear weapons. The exchange would have provoked the United States into retaliating, and World War III would have begun. The world would have been reduced to rubble. But because Kennedy didn't use violence against Cuba and made the Soviets remove those missile sites by peaceful means, the world was saved. Only John F. Kennedy could have done this. Any other president would have let the military exercise its might. But Kennedy used restraint, intelligence, and understanding to deal with this crisis.

So why would God let this great man be gunned down in Dallas that next year? Why wouldn't God prevent this astounding young man from dying in his prime? I think He could have stopped the assassination. This is why. John Kennedy was having affairs with many women. The FBI knew about them, and so did many others. Some of these women had ties to the Mafia. I don't give names because it isn't important. These women with whom John Kennedy was having sexual relations were about to come out and tell the media. If President Kennedy had lived, he would have been dragged down and humiliated. This would not be fitting for a man who saved the world from a nuclear war.

His dying on November 22, 1963, prevented this great man from being trashed by cheap, sleazy women and stopped opportunists in the media who were eager to write savory garbage and stories of sexual exploitation about him. The scandal would have ruined his presidency, tarnished his reputation, and given American a black eye. God would not let this happen to this great man. The country would lose a president but be stronger in the long run.

This was a time when the Soviet Union was trying to rule the world by imposing communist doctrine. The faith of the Soviets was at its height. Eastern Europe had been taken over by the communists, and all over the world where poor countries were struggling, communism was barking at their doorstep. Something needed to be done to break their faith and make them lose interest long enough for communism to fall apart.

When John F. Kennedy was alive, he wanted the United States to go to the moon by the end of the decade. I believe he wanted to do this to deny the Russians their faith in their ability to conquer another world. If the Russians had reached the moon first, it would have given them the faith to continue to conquer this world. Kennedy wanted to deny them this endeavor. And with his death, the United States worked diligently to reach the moon first out of gratitude for Kennedy.

This was accomplished on July 22, 1969, when Neil Armstrong took the first steps on the moon, with one small step for man and one large leap for mankind. Another thing happened that day.

The faith the Soviet Union had about conquering another world was destroyed. All that was needed now was time for the Soviet Union to realize that their world conquest crap was nothing but a doctrine of stupid rubbish.

Kennedy would help remove communism by words from his mouth. He became God's voice and with it did God's work. So you see, something good can come out of something bad.

Many things happen that are bad so other horrible things won't come to pass. During the 1960s and 1970s America was involved in a war that people didn't understand. This war gripped the United States like no other war; the war was in Vietnam.

When John F. Kennedy died in November 1963, Lyndon Johnson became president. Many people think Johnson was the worst president to ever hold the job. They think this because he got the United States involved in Vietnam. This was a terrible war that caused the deaths of more than 58,000 brave American sons. This war turned the country upside down. But what would have happened if Johnson hadn't gotten the United States involved in that confrontation?

One of the biggest fears back in those days was communism taking over the world either by force or by conversion. Anyway, it was real. The United States had to make a stand against it before it got too big to deal with. The fear of communism spreading to other countries had to be confronted.

If Johnson hadn't sent troops to South Vietnam, it would have been taken over by the North. That is a reasonable assumption. Then communism would have an unopposed gateway opened to push west and take over all of Southeast Asia. This would have resulted in many countries falling to slavery.

Could the United States just sit back and allow this to happen? Could the leader of the free world allow a large part of the world to be taken over without a fight, setting the stage for more countries to be conquered without lifting a hand to stop it? The world would have become a more dangerous place if nothing had been done. The aggressive communists would have become harder to fight with each and every conquest.

The more countries the Soviet Union controlled, the more faith it would have to continue to expand. Johnson knew this and tried to prevent communist expansion. His way to fight this war was wrong, and he failed. The North Vietnamese finally overtook the South and established another communist state.

But it wasn't a truly complete mistake on the part of Johnson or the United States to engage in a fight for South Vietnam. It is a fact that we lost 58,000 brave American soldiers and killed more than a million North Vietnamese, but if we hadn't fought this war, who knows what devastating events the future would have brought. Communism was contained and didn't expand in the region. Our actions did account for something.

In 1979 the communist dictator in Afghanistan decided he didn't want to be a communist anymore. The Soviet Union invaded that country and put in power another commie stooge dictator. Who knows, the United States might have come to their aid. I wonder how many US servicemen would have died trying to help the Afghan people. And to lock horns directly with the Soviet Union at that time in history could have been catastrophic. Who knows what would have come to pass with the anger of both forces trying to defeat each other. I am sure more than 58,000 US troops would have died. Who knows, nuclear missiles may have been exchanged. That is a frightening thought, but without learning from the mistakes of Vietnam, there is no telling what the United States and Soviets would have done.

To most Americans the war in Vietnam will always be considered a mistake. The war divided the American people like no other time in history. Many young lives were cut short. But if the war had been cut short, this would have given the communists more reason to grow. If we hadn't gotten into the conflict at all, who knows where communism would have gone. All of Asia would have soon been taken over. If America had left the conflict after making a stand to keep South Vietnam free, that would have helped communism grow throughout the region. Once a major power makes a decision, right or wrong, to engage in a conflict with its military, cutting and running only gives the enemy more faith and more determination to fight on and prosper.

There must have been a reason God allowed Bobby Kennedy and Martin Luther King Jr. to be assassinated in 1968. I don't know. Maybe some things happen that God can't prevent. But maybe ... just maybe there was a reason He allowed the lives of two of the greatest minds of the time to be shortened.

If Bobby Kennedy and Martin Luther King had not been killed, they both would have tried very hard to end the war in Vietnam. If the war had been shortened, many lives would have been saved, but ... it would have strengthened and given more credence to the communists of this world-domination doctrine. Who knows, if the war in Vietnam had been shortened by just a few years, Moscow may have branched out more boldly throughout the world, either by force or by corruptive methods. No one will ever know for sure, but one thing is certain: communism would have been strengthened, not weakened. Just think of what would have happened if the United States hadn't made a stand to stop communist aggression in Vietnam.

Many bad things transpire every day that can't be explained. It is something that should just be accepted so we can move on. God shouldn't be blamed for things that weren't His fault.

A lot of people have wondered why God allowed slavery to take place in America. Like, why didn't God put a stop to it? Sometimes God has to let things happen. It wasn't His idea for people to be put into slavery. The power of evil in this world works through the weakness of man. God inspires those obedient individuals to overcome the forces of evil and do His will. Those who do will be recognized as God's holy warriors.

To those African Americans who hate white people for bringing into being this horrible act of slavery, try to look at it this way: if slavery had never been instituted, the present-day African Americans would never have been born. Think about it. There would be no Willie Mays or Hank Aaron or Oprah Winfrey. The DNA that makes up these people would never have been generated! Their parents and grandparents and great-grandparents would have never been created! If everything in the past hadn't happened exactly and it did then all those people I mentioned would have never been born. That means they would never have lived in this world, and worse yet, never had eternal life. So think about that the next time Mr. Hate pays you a visit and starts poisoning your mind with his doctrine of racism.

As long as man can be deceived into doing things that are wrong, bad things will continue to happen. One must not blame God. I think nothing makes the Devil happier than tricking someone into doing something wrong and then getting that person to blame God. He then can use this person to do more bad things.

One should keep an open mind and try to understand that God has a long, drawn-out plan for each of us. We need to stay focused on what God wants from us. Think about what He wants and try to give Him your attention. At the same time, don't lose control of your anger. People make things worse when they cannot control their fury and rage.

The indignation of large groups only incites more and more hate. When hate is amplified, eventually violence will overflow. We see this in the Middle East and surrounding countries. More anger, more violence, more hate grows in that part of the world than any other. I sum it all up in one word: deception.

The Arabs want the Jewish homeland. This Islamic world wants the Jewish homeland. The Devil wants to destroy the Jewish homeland. That is why there is so much havoc going on in Israel.

The Devil has got to be put in his place. Peace will come to Israel—a peace that will last a thousand years. It will happen! It will come to pass. There will be a time when the Devil will not be allowed to deceive the Jewish homeland like he does today. Enemies will throw down their weapons and realize what horrible things they have done to each other.

They will embrace their foes with love and understanding. Only when the force field of hate is turned off and the window of deception is shattered will the world come together and become one; peace and harmony will be the norm. The Devil will be captured and imprisoned for a thousand years. For a thousand years mankind will prosper and rid this mean world of hunger, war, and hate. Time will tell. But I say to you, it will come to pass.

The Jewish people will be at the center of all this. It will be the Jewish people and their faith that will make this wonderful time come to pass. The suffering they have undergone and the sacrifices they have made will be understood, and a new beginning will begin.

To those who are going through hardship now or have been through a difficult time—there will be a new beginning for you also. Try to accept the things in your life. Don't blame God for everything bad that happens in your life. Look out for deception and try not to fall into its luring attractions. If you do find yourself committing wrong things, don't let your pride get in the way of admitting your mistakes. Life can be wonderful if your spirit is high and your thoughts are pure. Look for opportunities to make life better for yourself and for others.

You can be God's hands, so reach out and grasp the moment. You can be the answer to the suffering in this world. You can be God's feet, so run to the service of your fellow man. Your actions can change the world. You can be God's voice, so shout out loud that truth is the weapon that will defeat Satan. Remember, God is real. God is not to blame for the suffering in the world. He wants all of us to be happy, and we shall be if only we will do His will and show the world love.

You choose how you live your life. You can choose to live for God or the Devil. One day when your heart stops beating and your mind no longer thinks and your body dies, your soul will leave this world. You will then stand before the real God and answer for the things you did in this world, and for the things you didn't do that God wanted you to do.

The Devil will wait for you to run away from God and join his team. The Devil wants your soul, and he will get it only if you give it to him.

Life is a time to live and make real what God is. Your decisions are yours to make, for you will be the one who answers for them. You can do good things in this world or you can do evil things. Worldly gains can be accomplished with ease with criminal acts. Fame and fortune in the eyes of man is only temporary, but to be admired by God is forever.

Why does God allow bad things to happen? Why does man allow bad things to happen when he can prevent them? Why do bad things happen to good people? Why does man break the law to make his life easier? Why does God allow storms to destroy people's homes? Why does heat rise and move north? Why doesn't God do something about the violence in the Middle East? Why was this book written?

All the previous chapters in this book have been nonfiction. The truth has been written. I have attempted to show the character of the Jewish people, this humble people who only want to live and love and be happy. Only the last chapter will be fiction. Thank God it is only fiction. It would not have been fiction if God had intervened and stopped the mad dictator of the Third Reich. It is this last chapter I shall write, in hopes of telling the world why God allowed the Holocaust to happen.

God knows about the horrible suffering the Jewish people were fixing to go through. Before this planet was formed, the saga of what lay before these modest people, as well as their fate, was decided. God's hands were tied—tied with the rope of reality for the future of all mankind.

Lucifer had altered the world so that the coming of his son would play out to the end without any interference. The Antichrist would have his way, and death to the Jewish people would come. God knew that if He stopped Adolf Hitler from fulfilling his destiny, the world would meet a more terrible fate.

This next and last chapter will tell of this more terrible fate. It describes what would have happened if God had prevented the Holocaust. Maybe now the Jewish people can forgive God for what He allowed to happen to them. God knew the Jewish race, as a whole, would one day understand the reasons for Him allowing the Holocaust. There is something in the Jewish character that God understands more than anything else. They possess a special trait to love and serve God no matter what the consequences. Only when the ways of the world become more important than serving God is when they go astray and become bad. No race of people have had to endure more suffering than what the Jewish people went through during the Holocaust. It is now time to explain to the Jewish people and to all the world "why".

CHAPTER 9

The World As Scorched Earth

Let's go back in time. Way back. A time before TVs and computers were in every home. A time before CDs, PlayStations, and iPods were invented, back to a simpler time, when the world wasn't consumed with so many material things. And yes, a time before the thought of nuclear war was real. Yes! A time before nuclear weapons were ever created. The things that happened in the past happened for a reason. This is the time to tell the world why God allowed the Holocaust to happen. If things don't happen the way they did, the world have succumbed to being a scorched earth.

It is the eve of August 31, 1939. Adolf Hitler is fixing to invade Poland. The mad dictator waits impatiently, anxiety growing in his mind about what tomorrow will bring. He sits in Berlin confident about what his army will do to Poland. After stealing Austria and Czechoslovakia without firing a bullet, Adolf Hitler is ready to unleash his army and begin his violent campaign to smash the world into submission.

Now with Stalin's approval to invade Poland, he feels confident that he will overtake the weak country without much trouble. It was Stalin's permission to invade the country and his reassurance that he would not come to the aid of Poland that gives the mad dictator his confidence and faith that he will prevail in this, his first military conquest.

So on September 1, 1939, Adolf Hitler unleashes his army of 1.25 million soldiers upon the nation of Poland. There is no declaration of war, and the Polish people are caught up in a two-front war: Germany on the west and Stalin's army to the east. It takes only seventeen days for Hitler to devour Poland. An estimated 60,000 Polish troops are dead, 200,000 are wounded, and more than 700,000 are taken prisoner. Hitler and Stalin carve up Poland, and each take their share. Misery is everywhere for the people of Poland. Britain and France declare war only on Germany, not Russia. World War II has begun.

God with a heavy heart turns His head away from the carnage. He knows what lies before the Jewish people and the world. Lucifer smiles gleefully, showing a proud look as the German army is unleashed. He knows he has methodized the world so Hitler can execute his vengeance without interference. The determined, sinister grin shows an expression of total evil glowing in Lucifer's face.

The following is a dramatization of what would have happened if God had prevented Hitler from starting World War II. The only way He could have done this would have been to have had Adolf Hitler killed. God wouldn't have done this, for He is God, but I am sure His angels would have carried out the deed if need be. This is a fictional account of what might have happened if God had intervened. The reader should keep an open mind about what lies ahead. Would the outcome have been any different if Adolf Hitler had died earlier? Or would it have happened this way?

November 8, 1939, is a cold, rainy night in Munich, Germany. An audience has gathered to hear Adolf Hitler make a speech.

Hitler enters the loud, crowded room and begins to walk up to the platform. The room is filled to the max. A noisy audience waits to hear the Fuhrer give his speech. The room is thick with emotion and great excitement and anticipation. As he clears his throat, the excited people wait eagerly for his words. The crowd grows silent, waiting impatiently. Yet the Fuhrer waits until the entire room is quiet. He continues to wait. He waits until the atmosphere is at a fever pitch. Then the man begins. At first some meaningless words, mumbling and murmuring, exit his mouth. Then with a determined stare at his audience he begins.

This speech, like all the others, tells the German people to put all their faith in him and the Nazi party. He promises all things to all people, and of course he blames the state of the economy, the disgrace of the surrender of the Great War, and all the other hardships the country is facing on the Jewish people. The speech goes on and on. The power of his words seduces many in the audience with the enticement of a strange verbal sensation. His emotion and the delivery of his words transform the room into an uncontrollable frenzy. The power of his rhetoric is hypnotic and appeals to the minds and hearts of those who are here. He tells them just what they want to hear, and orchestrates it with a seductive power of emotion.

The speech goes on and on. Then something happens! An explosion takes place right where Adolf Hitler is standing. Chaos fills the room. People are crying and screaming. The foul stench of death and burning smoke fills the room. There lies Adolf Hitler, dead. His lifeless body, still and disfigured, lies dead on the floor. The broken body of the Fuhrer lies motionless for the last time. The blood and the smell of terror pour out freely into the delirious room of dispersed people.

Months go by after the assassination of Adolf Hitler. The politicians are in chaos again, trying to put together a new government. The communists are on the move, marching and chanting for their way of government. Time after time the communists pound their views into the ground. With money coming in from Moscow, they finally get their way.

They get most of the votes of the Reichstag. Then with a violent coup they take over what is left of the inept government. Hindenburg is assassinated, and all the Social Democrats are placed in concentration camps as are, of course, the remaining Nazis.

When word of the success of the takeover is broadcast in Moscow, Joseph Stalin is delighted. He immediately sends troops to keep the communists in power.

The world looks at the situation with disbelief. The British and French look at Germany with melancholy. They are glad Hitler has been killed but didn't want Stalin's communists to take over the government. They just look on with sadness for the rest of the German people, but there is nothing they can do. They just turn their heads and look away with a feeling of helplessness.

Months go by without any sign of war. Stalin's takeover of Germany slowly creeps into the consciences of the world. Slowly the people of Germany accept their fate. The German communist leaders rule with a tight fist. Anyone opposing the system is imprisoned or shot.

Czechoslovakia is next. In 1940 communist enthusiasts slowly manipulate the government. They get seats in their parliament, and the party grows bigger and bigger until one day another communist dictator makes a stand and takes over the government.

Soon after Stalin puts his stooge dictator in power in Czechoslovakia, he comes up with an idea to energize his schemes. He wants to make sure nothing goes wrong with his world-dominating plans, so he comes up with an oath all new communist dictators must make. He makes them swear to the death that communism will be the only form of government permitted in their countries. He brings to Moscow all those empowered by him to swear this new allegiance in front of the Communist Bureau. With this oath Stalin strengthens his grip on controlling Europe.

Germany is elected to be the driving force to spread communism to the small countries in Europe. Joseph Goebbels is made minister of propaganda after converting to the communist way of life. The propaganda he makes ready will soon poison the minds of the German people. Germany becomes the doorway through which to excel in this new way of life.

Many men get caught up in the lust for power they can achieve. They don't care what they have to do to get it. It becomes irresistible for many Germans wanting their place in the world.

Germany floods Europe with the communist doctrine like a tidal wave of immorality to these small countries. This in turn drowns their chance to save their freedom.

Not long after Czechoslovakia relinquishes its people to the communist doctrine, Poland, Hungry, Romania, and Austria do the same. Before the middle of 1940 rolls around, these countries are controlled by Stalin.

There are lies and more lies, and there's deception and more deception, until masses of people are enthused about handing over their freedoms for a plan for an easier life: a life where the government will take care of you, a life where everything will be taken care of, a life where there will be no worries about unemployment or how to pay for things like housing or medical care. The communists preach these things over and over again. "If you accept our way of doing things, then all things will be provided for you," they say, and the people accept this new plan. Germany is the primary driving force behind implementing this plan in Europe.

But there are a few who don't go along with this new paradise plan. Eyebrows are raised when country after country falls into this treacherous, devious new-way-of-life plan. This action gets the attention of the democracies of the world, mainly the US government. They try and try to get free elections and more freedom to the people, but with dictators at the helm, nothing changes.

Slowly Eastern Europe becomes subject to communist rule. The people of these once free democracies are enslaved by this cancerous germ called communism. It breeds slow and easy. It seduces the masses like a narcotic. The same ol' slogan is repeated time and time again that the government will take care of you. It will give you a job and a place to live. All the problems of life will be taken care of by the government. There will be no rich or poor. Everyone will live the same. This theory consumes the populations before they can realize what is at stake. Once communism takes over, there is no turning back. No way to change the system. The people turn over their freedoms for a system that will devour individuality and warp their character to belong to one system—one way of life, one way of thinking—and to be controlled by a system polluted with inanity, drudgery, and forced labor. People are told what to do. Freedom of speech and religion are not recognized or tolerated. You basically have to do what the leaders of the government want you to do. You can't leave the country for any reason other than what the government said.

But there is no war going on. The takeovers of these countries are domestic. By the time the communists have seized power, nothing can be done. If anyone intervened, they would look like the aggressor. Soon all of Eastern Europe is consumed by this newly man-made virus called communism. And these dictators get their orders from Moscow. Joseph Stalin holds the people of Europe in his tight fist and controls the souls of millions.

Eventually some people get tired of seeing their country being enslaved. Many try to leave, but the secret police intervene. Many are imprisoned.

The will to escape from this misery leaves many to perish at the hands of their own countrymen. The soldiers, police, and secret organizations control every aspect of the country. These small countries are controlled by Moscow—not by violence or aggression, but by ordinary men's lust and desire for power. Their appetite for worldly fame is traded for the freedoms of their own countrymen.

The passions of these dictators consume most of Europe. Like all evil things these men hide their sinful ways so the rest of the world will not know what is going on. The world with all its hang-ups simply turns its head and looks away from these communist countries.

By the end of 1940, Stalin holds Eastern Europe with an iron fist. He stays in full control of his satellite countries. His bloody purges continue to grow with the murder of many thousands daily, both domestically and abroad.

Anyone not following orders, or anyone conspiring to undermine Stalin, is shot. No trial, no place to plead your case or to be heard by any court. Stalin takes no chances; his ruthless actions are being carried out by men with no conscience. He rewards his subordinates with money, women, and vodka. Murder becomes easy for Stalin now. His word is law, and no one dares to oppose him—no one.

Converting small countries in Europe becomes easy once a dictator is in place. Stalin then starts to steal their raw materials and use the minds and the backs of the people to forge his way of life, and does so without much resistance.

This is done in secret, so the rest of the world will not see the evil being done. There are few protests to the treatment of these poor souls, as most protests would be dealt with domestically.

Money smoothes over things, as does the promise of powerful positions to those diverse individuals. Nothing is done to stop Stalin's thirst to rule Eastern Europe.

In this year, 1941, Stalin moves assertively to other parts of the world to entice more men to surrender their people's freedoms to gain supreme power for life. He branches out boldly and organizes a recruitment center to find selectable candidates to be reformed into his way of thinking. Countries in South America, Australia, and Asia bear the brunt of his actions.

He provides money, women, drugs, or any other substances to warp the minds of men and fuel their worldly desires to convert them under his control, and by doing so turns them into monsters.

The world continues to pay Stalin no mind. It is all done quietly and behind closed doors. Evil, like a virus, lives where it can't be exposed to the light of the world. It multiplies in the darkness along with the warmth of treachery and deceit. It grows and grows, and once it gets big enough, it devours the good and the righteous. Stalin's dark, sinister deeds continue to rob mankind of their freedoms without the conscience of the world knowing what is going on.

By the end of 1941, the world is still at peace. European countries quarrel about economic problems and inflation, but nothing big. Domestic squabbles consume most of the energies of the few free countries left. There are no risks of war breaking out. The communist countries remain quiet and hidden. The internal problems they face are smeared with lies and falsehoods.

Some in the US government have raised eyebrows about what is going on in these communist satellites, but without seeing what is really going on, they do nothing. They in turn give their attention to a growing threat in the Pacific: Japan. There is still no fighting in Europe. There is only peace for Europe at this time.

The growing confrontations between America and Japan begin to get worse. Japan's aggression in China is finally brought to the attention of the world. America continues to bring this to the deliberations with Japan. Japan talks only of peace, but its real intentions are of war and conquest.

On December 7, 1941, six aircraft carriers of the Japanese Imperial Fleet in the Pacific Ocean unleash 360 airplanes. Their target is Pearl Harbor. Without a declaration of war, notice of any kind, or any provocation, these planes bomb, torpedo, and destroy the harbor with a destructive power never experienced by any nation before. Thousands die, and many more are burned and wounded. Countless ships are destroyed. The entire bay feels the hate of war by Japan. The surprise attack sobers up the United States and makes us realize what Japan really stands for. The lives lost are avenged with a hatred of their own. This abomination done to them will be answered quickly with a force of a people united and determined to bring Japan to justice. The United States declares war and goes after Japan with a vengeance.

When word of the attack on Pearl Harbor reaches Joseph Stalin, he is delighted. Now he doesn't have to worry about the United States meddling in his affairs. He tells his comrades, "The Japanese will keep the Americans busy. I won't have to worry about them.

One day they shall fall into my outstretched hands like overripe fruit." Laughter fills the room as Stalin shows his proud look of delight.

While America prepares for war with Japan, Stalin has plans for the Middle East. He wants more countries to become communist. But he is having a problem with these countries. The religious nature of these countries don't seem to want to adapt to his plans very easily. Time after time he sends his agents to these countries, trying to win over someone who wants to be dictator for life. Religion becomes a brick wall in his way. It keeps interfering with his plans.

In May 1942 an incident gets the attention of the world. Nobel Prize winner Albert Einstein is killed while attempting to leave Germany. He is caught at a railroad station in Berlin, trying to flee communist Germany. He is spotted in disguise with a fake passport and tries to outrun the police, who have orders to shoot anyone trying to leave Berlin without the proper paperwork. He dies at a local hospital.

The door is open now about what is going on in Germany. The knowledge that people want to leave but are not allowed to begins to enrage the world. The government of the communist state tries to smear Einstein with allegations that he was trying to leave Germany because of criminal acts he committed. Nobody believes this, and the government gets deeper and deeper in trouble by adding lies on top of more lies.

In free countries committees are formed to try to see how people are living in Germany and why the government won't let people leave. A cog has been thrown into Stalin's machinery of evil. More and more people try to leave Germany. Some succeed and tell the world what is really going on there.

More and more speculation goes on about who is really responsible for deciding the policies of Eastern Europe. Stalin and the Soviet Communist Party Central Committee are bombarded with allegations from many nations of torture and murder inside the communist-controlled countries. Stalin gets fed up with these allegations and imposes sanctions on all of these countries. Before the year is out, Britain, France, and Spain break ties with Russia.

Stalin's easy road to control the world has met a snag.

When Einstein's body is taken by the authorities, they find many items very interesting. There are papers and designs of projects he was working on, even drafts of letters addressed to Franklin D. Roosevelt.

Before Einstein died, the secret police kept a close eye on him. They intercepted and confiscated many letters and important papers from the scientist. When collected these papers were immediately sent to Moscow.

After Einstein died more important papers were found. They also were sent to Stalin. He was very enthused about what he saw. Other Soviet scientists explained to Stalin what they were about. The papers were about nuclear fission—the act of splitting atoms, which would create vast amounts of energy. Doing so could create a very powerful bomb. Einstein wanted President Roosevelt to develop it before the communists did. These papers put into development the first nuclear bomb.

Other scientists were rounded up and made to work on this project, including German physicist Otto Hahn, who in 1939 split the first atoms and started the age of nuclear power; with his experiments with a synthetic element called ekauranium, he was able to create 200 million volts of energy. He and his subordinates were moved to facilities in Moscow.

Stalin wanted a special secret lab facility at which to develop this new bomb. He wanted it away from everyone else, where no one could interfere. After listening to his scientists about where a good location would be, Stalin chose a quiet area south of Siberia. It would be the perfect secret location for these scientists to work. Many more physicists were forced to work there. They had to decide to work there or go to a concentration camp. At first there was rebelling among some of the scientists, but with good food and luxuries such as beautiful women and pleasant surroundings, they slowly evolved and accepted living this pleasurable lifestyle. Afterward they did what they were told to do.

Stalin didn't spare any expense. Whatever money was needed, he gave the organizers; it was his concept of a blank check. Nothing was more important to Stalin than developing this new bomb before anyone else did. He made that clear to everyone.

As time went on, most nations didn't care what Stalin was up to. They were mainly caught up in the war the Americans and Japanese were involved in. Europe was still at peace and didn't want to involve itself with the Americans' problem. Many of the peoples in these countries were more concerned about their economy, day-to-day struggles, and just trying to get by.

A few politicians were concerned about what Stalin was doing. They did try to prevent any more countries from going communist, but their actions were futile and fruitless. The rest of the world turned a deaf ear to their voices.

By the middle of 1943, Stalin is ready to take some more countries by force. By the end of the year, he has aggressively taken many weak countries by violence. He has picked gentle countries that didn't want to fight. Easy prey was what Stalin wanted. Afterward he would install his stooge dictators in power.

When he gathered his armies up and invaded Finland in 1939, it was a cakewalk for the dictator. He took Finland with an overly powerful force. He then threatened to destroy their country if they didn't capitulate. The Finns' feeble fighting force was no match for Stalin's mighty army. He destroyed their armies and conquered their land. Now he wants to continue his aggression once again.

While the Americans are fighting the Japanese, Benito Mussolini of Italy is beginning to stretch his muscles again. He also wants to conquer lands that are easy prey. He moved against Ethiopia in October 1935 and took it over without much being done to stop him. His actions were looked upon by the world as those of an aggressive bully pouncing on a poor defenseless country. The formal emperor Haile Selassie went to the League of Nations to plead for help, but none was given to him. He left with bitterness and contempt. Now Mussolini wants to act on his aggressive nature once again and take over another country.

Mussolini is a great admirer of Joseph Stalin. He relishes how well he does things. He doesn't write or try to communicate to him because their governments are so diverse. He loves the way Stalin gets attention throughout the world. Mussolini wants to get some recognition of his own and feel like a big shot too. He makes a futile attempt to take over Greece.

His armies invade Greece in September 1943. They are repulsed from the very beginning. His army turns tail and runs back to a safe haven. Mussolini is embarrassed throughout Italy and the world. This failure cures his appetite for conquering lands from a people who will fight back. A revolt is started in his country. The dictator's days are numbered.

Very little is said and done about Stalin's acts of aggression. Before the middle of 1944 he has Georgia, Armenia, and Azerbaijan under his thumb. Also from the Black Sea northward to Finland his armies keep all these territories in check. They will move on a moment's notice if any coups take place.

The communist dictators Stalin put into power are now in charge of the police and army. They are ready to fire on their people without any consequences or any responsibility for their deaths. They simply call the rebellious ones traitors and then give the word to the police; machine guns curb their appetite for any freedoms they wanted. Killing the masses does not bother these men. Their minds are like robots. They would do anything they were programmed to do, even if it were to kill women and children. The leaders of the police and army are men with black hearts and lost souls.

As Stalin gets closer and closer to developing a nuclear bomb, word gets out that the Americans are doing the same thing. Stalin frowns at the news. He pressures his scientists to step up the pace on his plans for a bomb. He gives his scientists a deadline. He demands that a bomb be ready to test by the end of the year, 1944. His scientists are outraged at this demand. Some are executed by firing squad when they refuse to promise Stalin what he wants. He institutes a new wave of bloody purges. He demands complete obedience and will not accept any type of insubordination.

His secret police close down churches and synagogues in Russia as religion is outlawed. He doesn't want any religious beliefs interfering with his plans. His orders are to be carried out to the letter. His power is supreme. Nobody questions his orders; those who do are shot. Daily lists are made out of who should be shot. Many innocent people are put on these lists who have done nothing wrong. Stalin is obsessed with keeping control of his power. Killing an innocent man here and there only makes the Soviet state more secure by instilling fear in anyone wanting to overthrow the system. Millions are shot and sent to concentration camps all over Russia. People suffer terribly as the full power of Stalin and his evil ways are carried out.

People of the Soviet Union are so deceived about Stalin, they worship him like a god. All the misery he has imposed on them, all the hardships he has laid down on them, all the land he has stolen from them have been overshadowed by his deceptions. People in the concentration camps write Stalin and tell them of their misery and plead for him to help them. If they only knew that Stalin was the one who put them there in the first place. He is praised and adored by so many that no one dares to say anything negative about him. A picture of Stalin is in every household—a picture for the Soviet people to worship. He has become a king to his subjects—a king of evil.

By November 1944 Soviet scientists have finally come up with a bomb to test. The pressure Stalin has put on them to hurry up and develop a bomb has worked. The speeded-up process has produced a uranium bomb. The joy of seeing it ready delights Stalin tremendously. He wants so much to have a nuclear bomb ready before the Americans do. The test is for December 16, 1944, in a remote place in Siberia. Stalin is there to see this new bomb explode.

All the tests are made and the bomb is ready to detonate. Stalin, and some of his generals look on with great anticipation.

The countdown is made. Five, four, three, two, one. The bomb explodes but is a failure. The black mushroom cloud that is made is not what it should be. The fission doesn't take place. Stalin, not knowing one way or the other if it worked, simply grins. But when the chief physicists tell Stalin that the bomb didn't work and the test was a failure, he goes into a rage. He starts throwing chairs around the room. He goes ballistic. The generals who view this spectacle are at a loss for words. None of them dare to say anything, sensing that it might make Stalin even madder.

Stalin calls up a firing squad and has some of the scientists shot. He would have shot all of them if some of his generals hadn't stopped it. Stalin will not stand for failure. He wants the bomb to work and work right. He orders the scientists back to the lab to find out what went wrong and to make the next attempt a success. The remaining scientists are greatly intimidated to get another bomb ready, and they make sure it works.

Four months later, in early April 1945, another bomb is ready to test. Stalin is not present this time. He has made sure he will be told right after the test if it worked. He is eager to hear if the test is a success. He has many people photographing the explosion as it is set off.

The world press is there to document the event. People from all over the world come to see this event take place. Stalin makes sure the world knows what he has. He wants all to see. He wants to put the right manner of fear in the world if it works. He feels sure this time it will work.

The time comes. The bomb is elevated in a tower. Many workers surround the area where the explosion will take place. Cameras are focused on the sight with great interest. When the workers exit the bomb site, it takes on an eerie, cold, quiet feeling with a spooky silence. A chilly breeze blowing on the still tranquil test site brings a sense that something big is about to happen.

Soon the word is given and all go to a safe area to watch the spectacle that is about to happen. When everything is ready, the countdown begins. Five, four, three, two, one, kaboom! The light lights up the sky. The large mushroom cloud forms and a new era has been created. The time of the nuclear age has been born. Joseph Stalin has created the first nuclear bomb.

When word gets out, the world is mortified. The news spreads like wildfire. Every nation on the planet worries about what to do about this new destructive device. Stalin now has in his possession the most powerful bomb in the world.

The leaders of Britain, France, and Spain fly immediately to America to meet with President Roosevelt. They have to come up with an idea or a plan to deal with this most horrible event.

But as the conference takes place on April 12, 1945, the thirty-first president of the United States, Franklin Delano Roosevelt, dies. The world mourns the beloved president with a profound sadness. His death at this time only makes the current situation grimmer. The leaders of Britain, France, and Spain leave America with a more frightened outlook than they had when they arrived. What is the world going to do now?

The Americans are still working on their nuclear bomb. They are still months away from a test of their own, but the urgency to get one done is in effect. The plans to speed up production are top priority. They tell themselves that they must have one ready before Stalin uses his first one. Everything is done to speed up the work.

Harry Truman is now president. In his first address to Congress, he asks them to increase spending on this project. He tells them, "The world is counting on us to stop the Soviet Union from using this new bomb they have come up with. We must do anything and everything to stop communist aggression abroad. We must take the lead role in stopping Stalin and his desire to rule the world. We will win this fight!" Congress gives him a standing ovation with profound, jubilant applause. The determination gleaming on Truman's face radiates out a profound energy of strength and seriousness to all members of congress.

Back in Russia the men who worked on the development of the bomb are joyful and happy—not just because the test was a success but because they won't have to fear for their lives from Stalin's henchmen. They know now that Stalin won't kill them.

Stalin doesn't waste any time. He talks with his generals and figures out the best targets on which to use the bomb. What countries can he conquer now?

With most of Europe under his control except for Britain, France, Spain, and a few others, he looks south of his borders for some countries that will be easy to take—the ones close by that his bombers could reach easily.

He looks at Kazakhstan, Uzbekistan, Kyrgyzstan, Tajikistan, Afghanistan, and Iran. He likes the territory of Iran best. He thinks that if he could take a large country like Iran, the others would fall to their knees soon after. But to get to Iran he must go through Kazakhstan, then Uzbekistan, and then into Turkmenistan.

So the decision is made. Stalin's war machine is put into action. He mobilizes his army, and lightning warfare is unleashed on these countries. These small countries fall to Stalin like dominos. Nothing stops the mighty Russian army. His tanks cut through the defensive lines like a hot knife through warm butter. These three countries capitulate without his having to use his nuclear bombs. The three conquests take only four weeks. His armies are now on the border of Iran.

His generals proud of their accomplishments of these easy victories parade around with a glow of an evil achievement blazing on their faces; all worship Stalin like a god of war. They praise him and define him as the greatest military leader of all time.

It is now the beginning of June 1945, the warm season when flowers are blooming, the grass is green, and wildlife is abundant. In Moscow, there are celebrations everywhere. The city takes on the scene of a carnival. Flowers fill the streets, and people are joyous and ecstatic with excitement. Parades are everywhere.

Stalin is more a hero now than ever before. He makes sure the people have an opportunity to praise and worship him, but in the darkest corners of Soviet life, the bloody purges continue. Anyone saying or doing anything that would tarnish Stalin's reputation or the communist state is arrested and sent to a concentration camp without trial. Most are shot. Many thousands die every day at Stalin's hands. His ruthlessness and cruelty are at an all-time high. Nothing gets in Stalin's way. He is master of his own destiny. His word is law.

The God-fearing and the leaders of the church are tortured and murdered at Stalin's whims. He prevents the church from becoming anything with influence. He corrupts the leaders of all religious dominations to do what he says. The voice of the church has been choked and silenced. His intimidation of the church leaders works very effectively. The thought of being tortured warps the minds of many in the church to allow Stalin to continue with his sinister ideas. The chains of injustice and immorality have been placed on the Soviet people and the world. The world is now at Stalin's mercy.

Stalin plans to install communist rule throughout the world. He knows he is getting old. He makes plans for this design to continue even after he dies. He installs his son as his natural successor. He has been groomed extensively for the job. Stalin drives the concept of communist rule into his son's head. He makes sure that if he dies, the blueprint of the world as he wants it to be will be in place. His son does absolutely what Stalin wants. Now his vision will continue to grow even if he is assassinated or dies of natural causes. Others, many others, also have been groomed to continue to implement Stalin's dream.

God cannot change the course of events now with the death of Stalin. If He sends His angels to kill Stalin, there will be many more to fill his place. God is between a rock and a hard place. The Devil has put God in a stranglehold. The forces of evil have put a force field between God and man. God is now unable to change the outcome of what is about to happen. The world is at the mercy of Joseph Stalin and his dream of communist domination of the world.

It takes Stalin less than a month to get his army ready to invade Iran. It is now June 22, 1945. The word is given, and Stalin's army plunges into Iran. Fierce opposition is felt on the battlefield.

France, Britain, and Spain have tens of thousands of their own troops along with hundreds of thousands of Iranian soldiers on the battle lines. The Americans have sent some of their soldiers there also. Billions of dollars have been given by the coalition to the Iranians. The coalition is united to oppose the Soviet Army wherever it is. The cry to defeat Stalin is heard worldwide.

The strike has been anticipated by the Iranians, and the Soviet army takes on great casualties. Many thousands of Soviet troops lie dead on the battlefield. They manage to push through and gain ground, but the French and Americans push them back. The British, knowing what they are up against, lead an assault against the Russians with everything they have. They flank the Soviets and divide Stalin's army. Many are captured and many more surrender. The British celebrate a major victory against the communist war machine.

When word of the surrender reaches Stalin, he goes through a delirious fit. The tantrum he throws terrifies his generals and surrounding subordinates. He throws chairs at the walls and erupts into a raging maniac.

When he gets his senses back, he orders his generals to get ready to bomb Tehran. He gives the Iranians a chance to surrender. He will destroy their armies along with the French, British, and Americans if they don't capitulate. His last words on the document to the Iranian government are "Surrender or burn!"

The world sends diplomats from all over to persuade Stalin not to use the new bomb he has developed. The pope even intervenes to help with the bad situation, but to no avail. Stalin is mad. He doesn't look at the present situation with logic. He looks to use the bomb and take back his pride.

The Iranian government wires Stalin a response. "We will never surrender to you or anyone else. Our country is ours, not yours. You can go to hell, you fat pig!"

When Stalin reads the message, he goes into another fit. He loudly orders his generals to bomb Tehran the next day. He drinks a glass of vodka straight down. His numb brain and wicked thoughts along with his loud, angry voice mean he is about to embark on the Devil's work. Nothing on earth can stop the tyrant now. His word has been spoken. His orders have been made. All the angels in heaven can't stop the madness that is about to be done. God is unable to break the depravity of this evil.

On June 30, 1945, at 10:35 a.m. Iranian time, Joseph Stalin drops an atom bomb on Tehran, the capital city of Iran. The devastation is awesome! The large mushroom cloud is visible for miles. Eight square miles are completely destroyed! The splintered debris and broken glass fill the streets. The bodies of the dead create a sickening, burning stench everywhere! The city is destroyed!! Around 80,000 people are killed in seconds!

When the people of Iran witness this devastation, they look up to the heavens and cry out, "Why, God? Why have you let this thing happen? Why, God? Why?"

Word gets out about what Stalin has done, and the world reacts with protest and hate. They storm the Soviet embassies in many countries and kill the people in them. The revolt is everywhere—everywhere except Moscow.

The people in Moscow rejoice and praise Stalin even more. They worship him as a god now. His power over the people is complete. His orders are accepted without any delay.

On the battlefield there is still some resistance. Most of the Iranian generals still want to fight, but not all do. Those who do continue to battle the aggressor do so with a profound hatred and with total vengeance.

The British soldiers are told to come home. The French do the same. The Americans stay with the Iranians to do what they can. The situation is grim, but they remain to help the Iranians. They are the only ones who do. All others leave.

Most of the fighting stops. The Soviet army plunges through the disorganized enemy. The Iranians pull back as the Americans suggest, although they are eager to continue the fight.

Stalin attempts to install a puppet government once he has control of most of the Iranian troops. The rest have gone south to organize and fight another day.

The Russians take city after city without much resistance, but in the south a large Iranian army has been formed. They maneuver to a small unsuspecting Russian regiment and overtake them. Many Soviet forces die in the battle. All that are captured are tortured and then killed. None are spared. The madness Stalin has done to the Iranian countryside has been transformed to a madness of their own. The people rage in a protest of hate. Their hate is viewed by the whole world. They continue to fight! They continue to stand up to Stalin. The people rally behind the remainder of their army and cheer them for prevailing. Their determination is strong, and their anger is real. They chant, "Death to Stalin and to the communists." They show the world they have not capitulated. They continue to fight on.

Stalin, mad at the surrender of his troops, goes through another horrendous fit. He gathers his generals together around the room.

Charts and maps of the battle area are viewed closely in the semi darkened room. He talks with the stench of liquor on his breath. His generals and scientists look on with confusion and disarray. Stalin only wants to destroy and kill. He doesn't look at the current situation with a clear mind. The angry dictator consumes glasses of vodka while he listens to his generals talk.

He listens in a drunken stupor and with a mean look. He views the maps as he pours more of the clear liquor down his throat. One scientist tells Stalin they have only one more nuclear bomb ready. It is identical to the first one. They tell him it might be months before they can make any more. Then Stalin looks up in a quiet, tranquil state and says to himself, "One more bomb. It must be used wisely then." The look he has on his face is devious. His glassy-eyed stare startles the men. One tries to talk, but Stalin motions for him to stop. He then finishes off the clear liquid in the glass and says in a soft, lulling tone, "I want you all to listen carefully. I want to push all opposition to one area. From the far south region I want you to push the Iranians toward Shiraz." The warlords hold their breath as they hear Stalin's gentle tone.

"From the east and west I want you to push them also toward Shiraz. Do not capture the enemy. Let them get away." The dictator laughs a fiendish laugh as the others look on with intense curiosity. Stalin raises his tone as he points at the map. "But force them toward Shiraz. And from the north I want destruction like never before! I want death in every town and city. The remainders will go to Shiraz." More laughter comes from the dictator. Stalin then pours the remaining liquid from the bottle into his glass.

He throws the empty bottle to the side on the floor and with a gleam of evil in his eyes, says, "I want all opposition to find their way to Shiraz and then I will blow the city off the face of the earth!" Stalin bursts into laughter and the others in the room follow up with laughter of their own.

"I will destroy Shiraz like I destroyed Tehran. Then the world will do what I say." The men look at Stalin with fascination and intrigue. They bow to him, and some salute him. "Now, all of you get the hell out of here and do what I have ordered." The men with faces of excitement and delight hurry to exit the room.

By July 7, Stalin is ready to strike again. His generals push and force the resistant toward Shiraz.

The Iranians have formed a new government and disavowed Stalin's puppet government. The Iranians with conviction declare holy war against Stalin and the communists. The Americans are the only ones left supporting the Iranian resistance. They try to train and orchestrate a defense against Stalin, but with chaos and confusion all around, the task is difficult.

Stalin tells his generals not to attack positions where the Americans are. He doesn't want to ruffle their feathers and start any unnecessary confrontations with them. He gives word to the Americans to leave Shiraz. He warns only the Americans. The Iranians are still in the dark about what Stalin has planned.

Stalin leaks out to the Americans, the world press, and other local news agencies that he has fifty bombs waiting to be used against any resistance. He of course doesn't have this many, but he wants to give the impression that he does.

When word reaches Stalin that the Americans have left the city, he gives word to bomb Shiraz.

On July 13, without any warning to the Iranian people, Stalin drops an atom bomb on Shiraz. The city is destroyed. The aftermath is convincing to the Iranians now. The puppet government blames the resistance for the devastation of Shiraz, not Stalin. They order all resistance to stop. The ones who do not obey are imprisoned and then later killed. The puppet communism government is just as ruthless, and in some cases more vicious than Stalin himself. Soon there is no resistance left except a few guerilla groups in remote areas.

Stalin's plan has worked. Country after country falls to him like dominos. He orders them to surrender or burn. They all succumb to his wishes. Stalin has a free hand in that part of the world now. Nothing can stop him. His might is total and complete. The fear of destruction leads all countries to adapt to communism. No one dares cross Stalin now. He has complete power over this part of the world.

In Europe, Britain, France, and Spain are mostly the only ones left that Stalin wants to conquer. They have formed an alliance that they will continue to the bitter end to resist tyranny.

It is not only Stalin's might that gets these countries to fall, but the concept of communism itself. The people hear the words of the communists. Their words sound like paradise. "All your troubles will end. Communism is God's gift to the world. Stalin has been sent from God to show the world of this most wonderful way of life." At first the people are against the idea, but the seductive words flow like perfume into their ears. "You won't have to worry about where to live or what to live in. We will take care of that. You will have free health care and free schools and free food and free everything. We will take care of all your needs. We will give you a job and purpose for life." Slowly the people of these conquered lands eat up this talk and become enslaved in the promises the government makes.

To achieve all these things all you have to do is give up your freedom. The freedom to choose what life you want to live. The freedom to think for yourself. The freedom to worship God the way you want to. The freedom to be an individual and make your own decisions. The freedom to journey down the pathway of truth and happiness without being controlled by any other entity. To be free is what God wants for all of His children. Only the Devil wants us to be enslaved. And communism is the way to enslave the world without people realizing it. Then it is too late to do anything about it. The forces are too great to overcome. The complete goal of the Devil is to enslave God's world. His dream of total control is accomplished by communism.

If Stalin had had a heart attack, or stroke, or died of something else, there would have been someone else to take his place. The Supreme Soviet Bureau in Moscow would only appoint someone else as their leader. The thought of a world communist state would continue after Stalin's death. But Stalin isn't dead! He is now ready to take Britain, France, and Spain and make Europe his own!

The Soviet army moves on, taking country after country. The world rebels against Stalin with only words. More and more negative comments fill the Kremlin. Stalin's aggression has made the world tremble and allowed countries to unite against the communist menace. Stalin, seeing the world in such an uproar, tries to smooth over things with lies. He tells his ambassadors to stand up to the negative complaining they are hearing. Lies and more lies are told as Stalin continues to take over the world.

Moscow has taken on the scene of a carnival; people parade down streets while celebrations are everywhere. But in the dark, behind closed doors, Stalin continues his bloody purges.

Many tens of thousands of innocent civilians are murdered every day now. More than 10 million have been killed by Stalin. Millions more have been shipped off to Siberia to work in labor camps and starved. More blood is shed as the mad dictator continues his quest. His paranoid state becomes more and more intense.

Stalin thinks there are conspirators everywhere. He feels threatened by anyone who gets too popular. They are kidnapped and shot. He doesn't take any chances. Anyone who is a threat to Stalin in any way is eliminated. As the people of Russia worship their conqueror like a god, he in turns murders them with numbers never before known in the history of man.

Then something happens: on July 16, 1945, the world hears the exciting news that America has ignited a nuclear bomb in a desert in New Mexico. America has come into the nuclear age! The explosion is welcome news to the rest of the free world. Britain, France, and Spain send congratulations to Truman. They now have hope. But is it too late?

When the news reaches Moscow, Stalin throws a fit. He throws chairs at walls and once again goes into a terrible frenzy. He orders the messengers who brought the news to him to be shot. Military police carry out the task without any thought.

Stalin, with a worried mind, and disgust showing on his cold, aged face, asks himself what to do now. He is terrified upon hearing this startling news. He worries that the Americans will use this weapon on him. His paranoid state becomes so bad that he has a doctor give him medicine to numb his feelings. When he adds it to the vodka he consumes, Stalin becomes a disillusioned, chemical-induced monster.

With Italy in turmoil with the overthrow of Mussolini, Stalin chooses to leave it alone for now. The Italians are in no condition to overtake them.

In April of this year the people of Italy shot and killed the dictator after a quick trial. He was dragged through the streets and hanged upside down along with his mistress. Stalin knows the time is not right to negotiate any kind of takeover with Italy. In the back of his mind he fears this might happen to him one day. He is paranoid from the moment he wakes until he falls asleep.

Stalin hurries to take France, Britain, and Spain before the Americans intervene. He moves his army along the border with the help of the armies of Germany and other communist satellite countries. Knowing he doesn't have another bomb ready, he tricks the government of France into thinking that he does. He wires a message to the French government to surrender or burn. Paris is the city he threatens to destroy first. The French government at first says no, but a day later, after reviewing the devastation of Tehran and Shiraz, they decide to surrender to Stalin's armies.

Spain follows suit immediately after they are threatened. They are no match for Stalin and his new bomb. Communist dictators are installed in these two countries without delay.

Britain is the only country left that Stalin wants in Europe. He issues the same threat: surrender or burn. The British choose not to surrender. Churchill tells his people, "Never in the history of mankind has the Devil been so successful in deceiving the world. One man has a device that can intimidate and overthrow the free governments of the world and take away all the good things in life we hold dear. This man is after our freedom. But I promise you, our freedom is one thing we shall never surrender!" The people in Britain applaud their prime minister where they stand. Britain will not yield. Britain will not surrender.

On August 6, 1945, the United States drops the first atom bomb on the city of Hiroshima. Two days later they drop another, more powerful bomb on Nagasaki.

The Japanese surrender soon after ending the war. Peace finally comes to the United States and Japan. Now that the United States is finished fighting the Japanese, all efforts to stop Stalin are put into place.

Truman tells Churchill he will give him an atom bomb to protect his country, but protests from all over the world try to prevent it. Some in the United States don't want their government getting involved with Europe. They don't want to get involved with opposing Stalin. The people are tired of war and want to stop the hostilities. People have become naïve and frightened about what Stalin might do. People want peace and are ready to ignore the realities of the truth to get it.

Stalin doesn't want peace. He wants England to fall to its knees to him. He knows the longer he waits, the more opportunities Britain will have to get an atom bomb. He must enforce his demands and pressure Britain to capitulate as soon as possible. He thinks he can coerce Britain to fall before him. He gives Britain three days to surrender or be reduced to ashes. Britain gives Stalin no answer. They have chosen not to speak to the mad dictator anymore.

Truman warns Stalin that if he does anything to England, he will be held responsible and the United States will retaliate against him. Stalin throws away the warning. He is now so disillusioned with his drinking and drug taking that he thinks he can do anything. He thinks that anything he demands will be given to him. He has put so much fear into the world that nobody will dare oppose him. After the three days, Stalin, without another bomb, does nothing.

The rest of the world continues to protest against the Soviet Union and also the United States for using such powerful weapons. Weeks go by, and then months, as the world waits for the outcome.

Stalin grows impatient with his scientists for not having another bomb ready. He is angry that Britain hasn't surrendered to him and still worries what the Americans might do to him if he uses another bomb. His generals try to persuade him not to use any more nuclear bombs. They think that in time, England will be weak enough to take anyway. They fear retaliation from the Americans. Now that they have the bomb, they might use it to destroy their armies in Europe and abroad.

By the end of 1945, Stalin finally has another atom bomb ready. He knows now that Britain will not surrender his country or convert to communism. So on December 25, 1945, without any warning to the world, Joseph Stalin drops a more powerful atom bomb on London.

The world is shocked. All the peace talks that have taken place during these past several months have been in vain. London is destroyed. Without any warning, tens of thousands of people succumb to the blast. Prime Minister Churchill is killed along with the king and many more dignitaries. The unprovoked attack on London outrages the world. The Americans declare war on the Soviet Union the next day. Stalin must be stopped at any costs.

Now that a declaration of war has been made, it is only a matter of time until the Soviet Union and America go at it with each other. Nothing will stop the hatred. Nothing will stop the insane hatred these two countries have toward each other. Soon the world will be reduced to a scorched earth.

Epilogue

It began many billions of years ago when the universe was young.
A rebellion came to pass.
God and Lucifer made an agreement, and then the bells were rung.
So earth was created, and the angel Lucifer here he was cast.

Lucifer would become the Devil as his wickedness grew.
He plotted out a plan for man like the ingredients in a witch's brew.
The natural elements were created, and life began to form.
He waited for man so he could deceive and break God's scorn.

The world would evolve, and man would take his place.
The trickery of the mind slavery would be encased.
The harsh, cruel environment would only make the Devil's ways strong.
To institute the drudgery of hard labor—slavery—this would be wrong.

The Devil would deceive, and suffering would be at hand.
Turn mankind against each other would be the plan.
He would turn those most alike to conjure up hate, how ironic.
To make one feel superior would be the intangible toxic tonic.

The stage was set to see what man would do.
The ones the Devil would pick to unleash his evil would be in the stew.
He brought war and violence, and blood would spill.
The pride of life in mankind's heart is only what he needed to fill.

A man was born who became obedient to God like no other.
He was given the name Abram, and he would marry Sarah to be his.
The two were joined by God in holy matrimony to each other.
This man who acknowledges the existence of the one true God that is.

No children came from Sarah; she gave her husband none.
So Sarah gave Hagar to her husband so a child would be born.
God was not involved so the child, a bastard, he would become.
Ishmael was given as his name, which Sarah would soon scorn.

Isaac would follow, the son of Sarah and Abram.
Things would get sticky with Ishmael and Isaac like sugary jam.

A new world would emerge from these two
races.
They would quarrel and then be separated
and go to different places.

Isaac would marry Rebecca and have twin boys.
Rebecca would love both, but Jacob would be
her primary joy.
Esau and Jacob would be their names.
Through deceptive actions, Jacob would leave
because of his shame.

For seven years Jacob would toil to win the
love of his life.
He would be tricked and in turn mate with
Leah.
Rachel was Jacob's true love but in
strife.
He worked seven more years until his marriage
to her would be.

Jacob's name would change; he would now be
called Israel.
He would have twelve sons, and they became
the twelve tribes.
Here God would call this nation for his
chosen people Israel.
It would take David to come much later to
bring better vibes.

Joseph would be one of Jacob's sons. His
brothers would hate him.
They would beat and then throw him into a
well.
He would emerge and interpret Pharaoh's
dreams—all of them.
He would forgive his brothers for their
wickedness, do tell.

Moses would come and free the Hebrew slaves.
He would usher in ten plagues until Pharaoh would break.
Eventually Moses would win. He would win the day.
He would move his people away from Egypt that he did take.

The children of Israel would roam the desert for forty years.
Moses would be their leader. The Ten Commandments He would make.
The Israelites made a golden calf without any fears.
Satan would trick Moses, and the commandments he would break.

But the promised land would come to the people of Israel.
They have their country. They have their land.
Many would come, as the Devil would make them a deal.
To rob, kill, and try to bury the Jewish people's future in the sand.

A thousand years before Jesus, David would be born.
He would unite the tribes and be a light to the people as the sun.
He would be a rascal. His lust in his heart would feel like a thorn.
The desire for Beersheba to be his downfall would come.

The Jewish people have become a race but at the Devil's distaste.
Persecution would fall on them quickly and with great haste.

The world would turn against this humble
group.
The Devil would deceive. There was nothing
to which he wouldn't stoop.

Jesus was born, and the sins of all mankind
would be paid at the cross.
The Jewish people wouldn't believe. It would
be their loss.
The Devil would use this time to turn the
world against this people.
They became the scapegoat no matter how
strong or how feeble.

The Devil made ready to get the world in
the proper frame.
The Antichrist would be born. Adolf Hitler
would be his name.
Hitler would soon rule Germany as communism
slowly evolved.
He would be a disease to mankind as his war
machine would revolve.

Death and destruction would come to Europe
like never before seen.
It was the Jewish people he was after. The
Germans would be so mean.
Russia would be next. Hitler's war machine
plunged deeper.
Hitler devised a better way to murder—one
that was cheaper.

Poison gas from diesel engines would be
used. The plan was set.
Showers were told to the innocent victims
they would get.
The Jewish people now would die in large
masses.

The chambers were shut. Then they inhaled the poisonous gasses.

Oh, what a wretched time this is when innocent Jewish people must die!
Hitler would have his way. No one could stop the Holocaust.
If so, Stalin would be ready to take his place while his people did cry.
Because his wrath would devour the world and it would be a total loss.

A million Jewish people would be gassed, but Tehran would be saved.
Another million gassed in the chambers of death, but Mashhad is saved.
Another million die as the choking gas is unleashed, but Shiraz is saved.

Another million Jewish souls are gassed, but Esfahan is saved.
Another million Jewish people die from the gas as Tabriz remains free.
More will suffer and die. The torture! The agony! The misery!
How long can this madness go on? How long can this horror go on?
Another million Jewish people would be gassed, but safe is Tehran.

Those Islamic ones who hate the Jewish people have their reasons.
To the people of Iran, ask yourself in this new season.
Look at yourselves and honor those Jewish ones who died.
Your children are living. Your parents are living. You are alive.

You hate those who died for you. So open
your eyes and look at last.
The things that happened centuries ago are
long past.
God's chosen people were chosen to die so
the world would live on.
Now, where are the Jewish people in the
hearts and minds of Islam?

THE END

IN THE TREE BY THE BROOK THERE IS A SONGBIRD WHO SINGS
SOMETIMES ALL OF OUR THOUGHTS ARE MISGIVING